Living Well on One Income

IN A TWO-INCOME WORLD

Cynthia Yates

HARVEST HOUSE™ PUBLISHERS

EUGENE, OREGON

Cover by Terry Dugan Design, Minneapolis, Minnesota

Published in association with Books and Such, Santa Rosa, California.

LIVING WELL ON ONE INCOME
Copyright © 2003 by Cynthia Yates
Published by Harvest House Publishers
Eugene, Oregon 97402

Library of Congress Cataloging-in-Publication Data
   Yates, Cynthia, 1947–
     Living well on one income / Cynthia Yates.
       p. cm.
     ISBN 0-7369-1204-5 (pbk.)
     1. Finance, Personal—Religious aspects. I. Title.
   HG179.Y364 2003
    332.024—dc21   2003001889

To our grandchildren

Acknowledgments

Books aren't written in a vacuum. Experiences, encounters, and relationships pair up with native intelligence, schooling, and personal perspective. Add to that every magazine article or book read, TV show watched, or person consulted throughout an author's life.

While I do, indeed, possess skills and savvy to live well on *any* income—and the ability to write about it—I am the sum total of many other voices. I respectfully acknowledge and thank that collective anonymous mass of creative and professional people "out there" who have entertained and educated me along the way.

For those less anonymous...

I thank my agent and friend, Janet Kobobel Grant, Harvest House Publishers, and Gene Skinner (for his brilliant editing).

Again and again, I thank my mother, Alexandra, for drumming thrifty values into my corpuscles.

And in addition to thanking all of my family members and friends, I must issue an important disclaimer (since I don't want to be kicked out of the family or lose my friends!). Unless specifically indicated, I did *not* base any of the examples in this book on any of your lives whatsoever. I issue this disclaimer because what you may think is my bold reference to any of you is nothing more than my citing "average person" from "average street." Um...not that I'm claiming that you are only average. By no means! Ahem. I hereby attest that I am surrounded on all sides by amazing and talented family members and friends. (Am I off the hook yet?)

Special mention goes to my friend, Toan, owner of Charlottesville Coffee. You are a kind man.

Contents

To the Reader

I'm told that a good writer does not tell, but shows. This book does both: tells and shows. (Which, I suppose, leaves my writing ability in question!) From the philosophical to the zany to the mundane, I present to you my message of smart living on one income (or two, for that matter). From homespun sociology, to comedic hyperbole when sharing my many foibles, to practical money-saving and time-saving tips, Living Well on One Income introduces a sensible new voice in money management.

Consider this book to be your own seminar—just you and me in the privacy of your home. And here I am, standing in the middle of your living room, eager to share my method for living satisfactorily on *any* income. I may do something wacky every now and then just to get your attention, and I surely will repeat myself since repetition is such a good teacher. I may erupt in sarcasm over consumer glut. Yet, *always*, I will sound a cheer of encouragement for you as you face your financial dilemma with new resolve.

I will dance for you, do somersaults, fall on one knee, hop, skip, and jump for you. And then I will take you by the hand and lead you to the start of a new path, one that will guide you as you journey toward living well on one income, toward living with compassion for others, and at all times living to the glory of God.

CHAPTER 1

What's the Rub?

*N*ot enough money. That's the rub, isn't it? We Americans are having trouble with the bottom line. For many of us, our "income" is nowhere near as *incoming* as we'd like. A little more money would be nice—twice as much would be just the ticket out of our crisis and onto Easy Street. Yet for several reasons— not the least that *no one but you* can provide that elusive financial cushion—a lot of us confront our two-income needs clutching a single paycheck.

For some of us, the decision to manage on one income was made voluntarily. It sounded simple over a double-tall latte in the coffee shop...

> "I'm committed to you staying home with the children, Honey. I'll bring home the bacon."

> "Go ahead and get your degree! My job will support us both!"

> "Hey! No problem if your second cousin twice removed— and his family from *Poland*—come to live with us. My pay is enough to cover it all."

> "Go right ahead and follow your dreams, Love-O-My-Life. You *should* become the next Van Gogh (or Debussey or Streisand or Michener)."

"I fully support your tireless volunteer work with the disenfranchised among us."

"I am woman! I can pay for my mortgage, utilities, medical expenses, taxes, insurance, and living expenses on my own."

"I am he-man! I can pay for my mortgage, utilities, medical expenses, taxes, insurance, and living expenses on my own."

For others, the hard knocks of life landed on our doorstep before we could reach out and pull away our welcome mat...

"Please don't take your layoff so hard. It will be okay. We can manage on my salary." (With inflation out of the picture, and with no power to raise prices, companies see layoffs as one of the few ways to eke out profits. In the first three quarters of 2002, American companies cut 3600 jobs per day!)

"Don't worry about the medical bills. Your job is to get better. Let me do the worrying."

"We can manage on your retirement. We'll just send the grandkids a pack of LifeSavers and a coloring book for Christmas."

"Daddy is living someplace else now. But Mommy is here, and everything will be okay."

"Mommy loves you from heaven now. But Daddy is here, and everything will be okay."

Single wage earners abound. Frankly, many of us are living on one paycheck and don't even know it! In some cases, the cost of a second parent going to work far outweighs the benefits. A bewildering number of us are faced with the daunting challenge of living on one income. And we'd like to live well.

Living on one income in a two-income world can be like walking around with one shoe. The bare foot is uncomfortable, and stubbing your toe hurts. Many of us feel the bump of anger, depression, frustration, guilt—and if we're being brutally honest, envy—as our checkbook balance plummets while need and desire soar sky-high.

At other times, we feel as if we're trying to hitch a ride in the middle of the on-ramp of the Indy 500, bills and unmet needs whizzing by like a solid wall of 100 MPH traffic.

Slow down. Back up. Even though this book offers no free ride on Easy Street, it can lead you out of the traffic jam you are in. It will at least point you in the right direction. How will it do that? By showing you a new attitude, by teaching you a fabulous new creed, and by arming you with new skills.

The creed is a simple declaration of my belief that money and financial decisions are actually part of two economies: the visible worldly economy in which we live and the hidden but no less imminent spiritual economy of God's kingdom, both of which are manifested through His people.

The Creed

I don't want to be a tightwad or a spendthrift.
>   I want to be smart.
I want to celebrate life,
>   to surround myself with beauty,
>   and to be content in whatever state I am in.
I want to manage my finances,
>   to organize my routine,
>   and to use my possessions wisely.
I want to budget resources and time,
>   to help others,
>   and to bring glory to God.

These are the sentiments I live by, and you can, too!

Welcome to My World!

Over time and through determination I have developed a life of "one-income living with flair." It is a happy life packed with activity and surprise, a life honored with chatter and crowded tables. It is a life somewhat ordered yet delightfully spontaneous. It is also a life of interior peace because I no longer flinch when the phone rings or panic when the mail comes. Bills are paid and most emergencies are covered. What is more, I try to be sensitive to the needs of others and am often able to help out.

If this is how you want to live—in spite of your income—I offer you my hand in partnership. Let me share my system, a bit of friendly advice to help you to discover the inevitable satisfaction that comes from smart living.

Easier said than done? Not when frugal habits become second nature! In this book I will show you how to develop skills, attitudes, and goals that will bring you success. But first a few words of clarification:

1. Many people associate "frugal" with rock-bottom, threadbare, sacrificial living. I do not share those sentiments. *Frugal* means *smart,* not bare-bones fanaticism. (If you are down to bare bones already, I will show you how to find life and joy, even in your circumstance.)

2. This is not a book about investing or getting out of debt. A book on how to manage, save, and invest money should already be on your bed stand, underlined and dog-eared. This book is a crash course in what may be a brand-new perspective for many of you: *smart thinking.* My principles will help you cruise toward debt-free living if that is your goal. Once these principles become habits, you will naturally...

   ▪ save bundles on groceries

   ▪ dazzle guests with the simplest and most economical meals on earth

- live peacefully with your former enemy—time

- put pizzazz in your palace and pocket some change

- give gifts from your heart that don't empty your wallet

- outsmart catalogs and Internet promotions

- find the best buys in *any* store (yes, even auto parts)

- quit worrying, live more, give more, splurge a little, and save a lot

The Adventures of Frugal Woman

We learn by example, so I will try to inspire creative thinking in *you* by telling much of *my* story. This book is crammed with anecdotes of victories and blunders from my own journey toward the smart and frugal life. Some of my escapades are funny, like the night of the slippery sheets; some are silly, like the daring dumpster rescue; some are sad, like the story of the Russian Babushkas. All, I hope, are instructive. Let's start with a recent revelation that occurred in our living room.

That Stupid Couch

It was an outright epiphany. The discovery came to me midconversation with my husband, Joseph. "Hold that thought!" I yelled, as I jumped from my chair in one decisive maneuver, grabbed our big, ugly throw pillows, and flung them downstairs. *That was it!* The problem with the couch—and therefore the living room, and therefore the entire house, and therefore my *life*—was the ugly throw pillows! That stupid couch had bugged me for three years. I was excited; once I tackled the cushion problem, everything would be perfect!

Our couch is well-crafted and strong, a brownish beige tweedy behemoth in the center of our living room. It may *look* okay, pillows aside, but it is all wrong. Specifically, its seats are too deep for anyone but a professional basketball player. When I sit on our couch with my spine quite properly against its backrest, my feet stick up as they did when I was a kid and got swallowed in the yawning maw of Mrs. Galka's sofa with my patent leathers pointing north.

Our backrest is divided into two poochy sections that look nice when punched into submission but deflate into a groove the minute someone sits against them, pushing the seat cushions forward. That is why the couch came with four big, raspberry-ripple pillows—so normal feet could reach the floor. And there's more.

Namely, the feet on which this couch stands are covered with the same brownish beige tweedy fabric, which means when someone leans against it, it slides over our wood floor. This design fault was tragically learned one Christmas Eve when someone in our overflow crowd leaned against the couch, sending it and its occupants clear into New Jersey.

This couch had been a real problem—and then my epiphany: *Why hadn't I seen it before? Those cushions not only clashed with the rich colors and style of our rustic "Old World" decor, they clashed with the couch!*

Once I replaced the cushions with something classier, something softer, something *smaller*, the living room would look quaintly country-French, people would revel in their comfortable surroundings, and life would be A-OK.

Couches "R" Us

What does all this fuss about our couch have to do with smart living? Plenty. By taking an honest and humorous look at my angst over four ugly cushions, we see a reflection of our souls. And what we see is clear: We are never satisfied. That is why some of us are unsettled, why many of us face discontentment, and why many of us spend. *If I can get that one more thing...replace those four cushions...then life would be A-OK.* Until the next epiphany.

Why are we like this? Why do we need that *one more thing?* Why aren't we satisfied with what we have? And why, in spite of my own philosophy toward life, do even I find myself restless and in need of a spending fix from time to time? It's called *programming*—and we've been programmed since infancy.

Cartoons have become half-hour commercials for toys and cereal as the lure and promise of true happiness reaches out to younger and younger children. Adults watch clever infomercials with rapt attention. Men in chef hats tell us to buy pots and pans, glamorous women tell us to buy makeup, famous golfers tell us to buy motor oil. And we obey. We have become a nation of obedient consumers, sipping designer coffee, our designer to-go mugs clutched in one hand, our cell phones in the other.

This is partly because the folks who work in advertising agencies know something that many of us don't: We Americans find identity, satisfaction, and worth in what we buy. Who we are has become wrapped up in product identification. We wear labels like scapulars, shopping with religious fervor; we wear labels like badges, the right shoe or tennis racket giving us a positive edge; we wear labels like medals, flaunting our prominence among others.

First on radio, then on TV, and now on the Internet, we are blasted with a constant message: You *thought* you had nice cushions before, Cynthia. Wait till you see them new and improved! Think how they will enhance your life!

Day in and day out each and every one of us is tempted to fill our lives with the distractions of this world at the expense of our relationships with God and neighbor. We have been masterfully manipulated to nurture our neurotic compulsion to buy.

- Do not be satisfied!

- Our product is guaranteed to fix your problem!

- Listen to what others are saying!

- Imagine what others will say or think about you!

- You have to have this!

- Why wait?!

Wait long enough to visit and enjoy a cup of coffee with a companion? Wait *long enough to park* before we make a phone call? Wait long enough to sit on a couch with ugly cushions to listen to music or engage in conversation? Why should we wait? Our need to be new and improved has translated into not having to wait. We need our gratification fix, we need it now, and we have the means to get it. (*Paying* for it is another story.)

In the economy of God's kingdom, we must ask ourselves what impulse is driving this need. We must reclaim a serious engagement with this impulse if we are to adequately understand—and satisfy—that impulse.

Madison Avenue has strategically fostered ego gratification through its products: *I just know that if I have a famous-name measuring cup I will not only cook better, I will be just like the woman with the famous name. I just know if I wear a certain brand of sneakers I will jump sky-high or win the match and be just like the athletes who hawk those shoes. I just know if I have the same tool as the man on PBS I will build great things, and I will wear a flannel shirt when I use that tool to boot, just to be like him.*

Never mind the famous woman, never mind those athletes, and never mind that tool guy. Better you should emulate Gram and Gramps.

> *Smart Think:*
>
> Do I want my identity to be reduced to my consumer preferences, or do I want my identity to be rooted in Christ?

To Grandmother's House We Go

Some of us remember the predictability of a visit to grandma's house. We would sleep on the same sheets on the same bed and drink from the same glass and eat from the same plate and play the same card game. Visit after visit, year after year. There was sameness, normalness, and, might I add, contentment—for us as well as for Gram and Gramps. Our grandparents were satisfied to have the same homemade macaroni and cheese on Monday night, to wear the same dress clothes on Sunday morning, and to drive the same old sedan into town. In other words, our grandparents *made do* with what they had. And for the most part, when something new came to the house, it was bought and paid for. Thus the excitement (sometimes for the whole neighborhood) when a new Maytag or color TV was carted home.

We would be foolish to extol many aspects of our grandparents' lives. Technology, the computer age, medical advances, and other changes in our lives are undeniably progressive and mighty helpful. We should never be afraid to break new soil and face the beyond of any untried road.

What we should extol are the virtues that drove our grandparents. Virtues that seem to have been left under the doormat when progress came knocking at the door.

Easy Credit Knockin' on Your Front Door

If easy credit came knocking at Gram and Gramp's door, would they have gotten up to answer?

It was right about the time Gramps was settling down to snooze his way through retirement that progress came calling with easy credit in tow. Credit that was initially designed to jump-start our sluggish economy became an industry unto itself. "Buy now, pay later" became the mantra of excited consumers who could have just about anything their hearts desired without sacrifice or second thought. Madison Avenue was smacking its lips. And why not? Instant gratification fit nicely with grand plans for personal fulfillment. "Drinking glass?! You should have one in every color! Why worry about the pileup in your sink? We'll sell you a dishwasher! And then we'll invent improved dishwashing soap! And stuff that makes your glasses sparkle! See how much you need us?!"

> **Smart Think:**
>
> Ever roll a nickel on its side? What happens when it slows down?

And so, while Gramps snoozed, we went on a roll.

Credit now drives our economy. Espresso, a night at the movies, pizza, cab fares, tax bills, college tuition, measuring cups, and yes, new couch cushions, are just a swipe away as we whip out our tiny piece of plastic and make everything A-OK. At least until we come to our senses and recognize that credit-card accounts are designed to keep us in debt forever. That's how they make their money and stay in business.

> We ought to change the legend on our money from "In God We Trust" to "In Money We Trust." Because, as a nation, we've got far more faith in money these days than we do in God.
>
> —ARTHUR HOPPE

Don't Charge, Take Charge!

Some of us are in a predicament, a precarious position where survival is wholly dependent upon one paycheck. Some of us have managed our money fairly well, but we can't seem to get a leg up on savings. Also, for as many reasons as there are drops of water in the ocean, some of us are struggling to stay afloat.

And our boats are floating on very troubled waters right now. America faces threats that affect our wallet every single day: stock market destabilization, recession, inflation, trade agreements with less developed countries, corporate downsizing, unemployment, and soaring energy costs (which will affect everything but breathing, and that only if you are not on oxygen). All contribute to real concern about our financial future. (Not to mention our financial *present.*)

Are we culpable in any of this? Do we bear any responsibility for our dilemma? Some of us do. Programmed or not, no one held a cash register to our heads and forced us to buy anything or to mismanage our funds. Most certainly, some people are having financial difficulties as a result of another person's actions or because of unfortunate turns in life. Not everyone who has ended up on the short end of a paycheck has brought misery upon himself or herself. If some of us "fess up," however, we will admit that gluttony, pride, covetousness, insecurity, jealousy, addiction, and selfishness have contributed to any predicament we are in as individuals or as a country. The truth is that God deplores all selfishness and expects us all—rich, poor, middle income—to live unselfishly within reasonable means so that no one lacks such basic needs as food, shelter, clothing, and medical care.

So What Do We Do?

Here's the good news: Learn and appropriate ten principles of smart living and you can have your double-tall hazelnut latte and drink it too! (Just maybe not as often as you'd like.)

Let me make something clear: *The purpose of this book is not to avoid consumerism but rather to promote a new approach to consumerism.*

Remember Gram in her kitchen washing those same old dishes and Gramps in his lounge chair sawing logs? They had something we don't. They had thrifty skills and knew how to use them. This is the primary issue. Our grandparents practiced skills that we do not. Though older mores are not popular in today's climate, we must recover and appropriate them for today. (We must, however, also bear in mind that Gram and Gramps had a different occupational reality. Most of their contemporaries spent their lifetimes with a single employer, and very few needed advanced education.)

Many of us have simply never learned *how* to be frugal (excuse me...how to be *smart*), and many of us feel we don't have time. Can old-fashioned grit and determination be applied to our insanely busy lifestyles—lifestyles that include little patience for anything that isn't speedy and convenient? You betcha!

I've lived by these principles for years and consider my life "frugal with flair." Do I have designer coffee beans in my freezer? Yep. (Learning how and where to store those beans is an important skill.) I also have good, organic olive oil, give awesome gifts, host fabulous parties, take an occasional trip, pay all of my bills, and have the wherewithal to replace those ugly cushions. And by the way, I do it all on my husband's (average) income. Let me tell you how.

Frugal Means Smart

If you learn anything from this book, learn this: *Frugal means smart.* Years ago, many pleaded the case for thrift, but I squirmed at the thought of being a tightwad, skinflint, miser, cheapskate. I didn't *want* to be as tight as the rubber band on broccoli. Those books gave good and necessary advice, but it was under an umbrella of guilt if we didn't make our own soap or change the oil in our own cars. (Not that those aren't good skills.) *Time* to do these things became our mortal enemy. *Inclination* to do these things was fleeting. Some of us tried and failed, spending more, I might add, buying all the tools and equipment to fulfill the tightwad mania that was sweeping the country. We soon became disillusioned, gave up, and resorted to old spending habits.

Well, here comes a news flash: *None of us is perfect.* Isn't it about time we acknowledged that? This book does not present a picture-perfect scenario: Do *all* of this or that and life will be carefree. That would be irresponsible and simply impossible. Can't be done. Too many bumps and too much human nature in our way. What this book *does* do is plead with you to adapt certain strategies that will give you small victories within your limited income. Over time, each victory will bring you closer to transformation and greater satisfaction—satisfaction guaranteed.

When I stay on the track of my specific guidelines, I am satisfied. Satisfaction comes from my sense of accomplishment, my power over Madison Avenue, and the fun of tackling my latest challenge, whether it is hosting a Mexican fiesta for six, outwitting the energy ogre, or figuring out what to do about the couch.

Frugal does *not* mean...

- I don't want to improve my surroundings.
- I don't want nice things.
- I am any less influenced than others by decades of conditioning through crafty ads, pitches, and promises.
- I live in a cave and trim my candlewicks.
- I eat gruel with an occasional dollop of home-made jam.
- I look bad or smell bad.
- I must be a grump!

Frugal *does* mean...

- I am patient and rarely allow impulse to rule.
- I shop intelligently and buy sensibly.
- I become savvy by *listening* to the crafty pitch and by *studying* the catalogs.
- I love my surroundings and get excited planning new projects.
- I eat wholesome food and set an awesome table.
- I have a closet of excellent clothes (that don't smell).
- I am a satisfied person!

Ten Ways to Outwit the Couch

What probably set my mind in motion about the couch were the gorgeous throw pillows I saw at a warehouse store. Very old-world, the pillows were soft without losing shape and smaller than the big, stiff purple blotches we had and they would add a stunning accent to the room—at $14.99 each. What to do?

I could *adjust my attitude* and be patient until I come up with a good idea or stumble onto something besides the warehouse store pillows. Or I could be satisfied with the pillows that came with the couch. Bleagh.

If I bought two warehouse pillows, I could easily stay within our monthly budget for household improvement, and therefore *live within my means*. But first I had to apply a few thrifty habits. What if I *organized* my house and looked for possibilities for cushions from other rooms? How *savvy* would I be if I made new pillows? In other words, what if I *rolled up my sleeves* and borrowed my mother's sewing machine? By the time I bought fabric, even if I am savvy, the savings might not be worth the effort. Hmmm...Do I have any fabric on hand? I could *use things up* and put my leftover olive green fabric to work as a backing for each pillow, and if all I needed was a front piece of fabric and some stuffing... I should be able to find something on sale or even use an old print blouse, or how about a pillowcase or sheet? Nah, we have only two sets of sheets for our bed, and both are white.

Not wanting to *waste* my *creative genius,* I might be able to recover those purple eyesores, especially if I could stuff them into a colorful pillowcase. But I'd still have the "big" even though I'd gotten rid of the ugly.

Presentation matters to me, so whatever I do must be carefully thought through. So out goes impulse. In the meantime, I will be thankful that I even *have* a couch and therefore *honor God* for His blessings.

And there you have my guidelines, your new principles for smart living:

1. Adjust your attitude.

2. Live within your means.

3. Organize your world.

4. Learn prices and become a savvy consumer.

5. Roll up your sleeves.

6. Use things up.

7. Do not waste.

8. Use your creative genius.

9. Presentation is everything.

10. In all things, honor God.

This book is filled with whimsy, a bit of serious self-reflection, and so many practical facts and helpful ideas they're fairly falling off the pages.

What you are about to read is my philosophy (replete with successes and failure), along with nonstop encouragement for you to live well on *any* income, to live to God's glory, to live with gusto, and to enjoy more on less.

CHAPTER 2

A Cheerful Heart: The Right Attitude

The Adventures of Frugal Woman

Nothing would put more spark into our love life, I reckoned, than a new nightie. So into town I went, my dented silver "beater" coughing to catch up as my foot pushed against the gas pedal. I was on a mission.

Our local thrift store gave me a royal welcome. There I found a long, teal green number, a slithery thing with poofy sleeves that snapped tight above both elbows. Knowing teal to be attractive on just about anyone, I plopped down $2.29 and headed straight home to our laundry room. The stage was soon set.

"I'm coming, Wonder Man!" I called as I stuffed myself into my new nightie. It sure was snug. It sure dragged on the floor. Those sleeves sure were puffy. Maybe I should have tried the thing on...

Joseph stared in utter astonishment when I duck-walked into the bedroom, the nightie too tight for anything but a waddle. There I stood, The Queen of the Dorks. Husbands take note—the poor man actually complimented me. Sort of.

"Um," he said, "teal is definitely your color…"

Now, because I am on the customer "A" list at the thrift store, I have return privileges. (If frequent flier miles were awarded at this place, I could fly round-trip to Pluto.) Back I went, disaster nightie in hand. In exchange, I bought two baskets with $1.29 to spare. And then I saw it: a peach cardigan in mint condition— a *designer label* peach cardigan—for $1.29. Sold! Later that day I stuck my hand in its pocket and pulled out the retail tag: $150.

The Right Attitude

The story above has little to do with driving a dented car, looking for treasure at a thrift store, or having a sensible return policy. It has to do with an *attitude*. In my case, an attitude that is not a bit bothered to drive a dependable used car, to haunt thrift stores, or to return something that does not serve its intended purpose.

In *your* case, the bald truth is that *nothing* will help you to live well on one income unless you have the right attitude. For some of you, that may mean a major adjustment. If so, be prepared: Attitudes about money management need adjustment just about every day.

The financial whiz kids tell us most money messes have more to do with spending than with income. Most of us probably know this, but the hectic pace of life provides us with little time to slow down and figure out a new game plan. A change in outlook can help you gain without too much pain. Changing your perspective can put extra change in your pocket for sure, but that change will not come without daily fine-tuning. In fact, until you get steady legs under you, you may fall down as often as you pick yourself up. Why?

Temptations rarely self-destruct, poor habits die hard, and unmet needs from deep inside that hunger for fulfillment, meaning, and material comfort all tend to linger. As soon as your guard is down, *pow!* There they are again, like a palooka punch to the pocketbook, until they are finally tamed. Demands of family, pressing bills, and dashed dreams loom larger and larger, and before long each blow sends your mind reeling and your emotions spinning.

Yippee-Skippee

A right attitude does not mean yippee-skippee; it means that you have chosen to courageously face your situation out in the open, to *confront* your predicament head-on.

Each of us could recite a long list of sugary ditties that the rah-rah bunch has foisted on us: Don't worry, be happy; let a smile be your umbrella; make lemonade from lemons. We need more than a cute slogan to help us overcome unproductive thinking. Frankly, there may be times when you feel as if *nothing* can change your outlook! We will talk about that soon, but in the meantime, the bottom line is that the wrong attitude will sink your ship faster than a cannonball from the S.S. Doomsday.

Smart Think:

Frugal living, smart living, living within your means, liberated living, and peaceful and abundant living will not happen without the right attitude.

The Adventures of Frugal Woman

I was presenting a workshop at a retreat. During the break, a woman approached me. She was clearly a woman of little means, but the story she shared with me brought me near tears. Here is what she said:

I was in the mall with my husband, and we didn't have any money at all. We were just killing time, really, and keeping warm. Both of us were sad because it was our anniversary.

At one point my husband said he'd be right back and left. Later, while I was looking in a store window, he came and grabbed my hand and pulled me toward the card shop. He hurried me through the crowded aisles and stopped in front of the anniversary cards. And he was beaming. He reached down and picked the most beautiful card I'd ever seen, one with colorful raised flowers and with very loving words.

"If I could afford a card for you, Honey," said my husband, "this is the one I would buy."

What an attitude that man had!

What Is Your Attitude About Money?

- Money is a tool I use to control or manipulate others.
- Money is a means to satisfy emotional hunger.
- Money is a fix for my latest disappointment.
- If I get enough money, I can buy happiness.
- The love of money is a root of all evil.
- Money is a reward, and I should use it accordingly.
- Money is merely part of God's providence, for which I must be a faithful steward.
- Money enables me to help others.

The Water Glass

Did the man in the card shop see his water glass half empty or half full? People generally fall into either category: Some are pessimists and some are optimists. Some go to extremes: those whose glasses are utterly empty and cracked, and those who regard even an empty glass with excitement— why, *think* of all the things with which it can be filled! Filled to overflowing! Yet, sometimes, life gets to even the most positive among us.

Tired of Trying

How many books have you held like this? Books that promised to help, that promised the newest method to lift you out of despair, that guaranteed you would lose weight, save money, grow a perfect garden, become a man or woman of valor, pray correctly, parent your children correctly, love passionately? I'm guessing this is not the first self-help book in your library. We all come along, don't we, and promise to make your life better, easier, worry-free, and meaningful. And oh, how you have tried! With each new system to hit the bookstores and the talk shows, you've put your foot on the accelerator and revved your engine for success. Easy Street, here I come! What happened next?

Many of you went back to old systems, old patterns, old habits. That is because, as I've mentioned, habits die hard. And like the demons who were swept from the man in Matthew 12, old habits must be replaced by new habits or they will come marching into your life again, swords rattling, to reestablish their stronghold.

You may have failed so often that it is hard to muster enthusiasm over *another* agenda. Could failure have been tied to wrong attitude? And could the right attitude have prepared and cushioned your bruised ego for some predictable bumps along the way as you committed yourself to transformation?

> A miserable heart means a miserable life;
> a cheerful heart fills the day with song.
>
> —PROVERBS 15:15 (THE MESSAGE)

Revolution

When our son was ten, he welcomed one New Year's Day with a smudgy list of "revolutions." Charmed by his boyish blunder, our household has traditionally written New Year's "revolutions" since.

Some of us would *need* a "revolution" to change perspective or attitude. The reality is that all of us have to go through our own "revolutions," and pretty regularly at that, in order to win this battle for financial stability and security. A battle, I might add, that we fight shoulder to shoulder with everyone around us.

For the same reason we resolve to improve the same areas of our lives *over and over and over*, year after year, we must routinely resolve to meet our money challenges head-on. This involves a lot of recommitment and is something all of us must do, even those of us who write books.

Developing new habits and a new outlook is hard, but it is the only logical choice when faced with other options: constantly struggling to make ends meet, growing weary of going without, being filled with fear over the situation you are in, wishing for a little breathing room. That may be how you live your life now. My question to you is, What on earth for?

Life is hard. And that is exactly why attitude counts. A right attitude, even in times of struggle, weariness, or fear, can make a cheerful heart and lead to biblical joy.

Rejoice

The Bible tells us to rejoice always, in all things give thanks, and again it says rejoice. Joy in the morning, joy in the evening, make a joyful sound...this from psalmists who definitely knew their share of trouble.

Listen to the despair of David, who sent an urgent SOS to the Lord of refuge:

> Be merciful to me, O LORD, for I am in distress;
>   my eyes grow weak with sorrow,
>   my soul and my body with grief.
> My life is consumed by anguish
>   and my years by groaning;
> my strength fails because of my affliction,
>   and my bones grow weak (Psalm 31:9-10).

Hoo boy! Talk about depression! Yet David also writes:

> We wait in hope for the LORD;
>   he is our help and our shield.
> In him our hearts rejoice,
>   for we trust in his holy name (Psalm 33:20-21).

Again It Says Rejoice

Read the start of Romans 5 and see what Paul has to say about rejoicing in hardship. Note his words carefully: We should rejoice *in* hardship, not *because of* hardship. Big difference! How on earth can we do that? We can do that because through Jesus Christ we are ushered into the presence of God, says Paul. That's got to make *anybody* joyful.

Scripture tells us that joy is a gift of God that can be experienced even in the turmoil of adversity. Joy is not just an emotion. Joy is an inner quality that is a vital part of our relationship to God. "The fullness of joy," says my fat Dictionary of Theology, "comes when there is a deep sense of the presence of God in one's life." Psalm 16:11 says: "You have made known to me the path of life; you will fill me with joy in your presence, with eternal pleasures at your right hand."

A Christian, in particular, clings to the joy of resting in the promise and love of God. That makes for a happy heart, indeed.

Rejoice with Those Who Rejoice

TV therapists tell us that we should not depend on others for our happiness, that we alone are responsible for our happiness. To that bit of psychological wisdom, I say *phooey*. Saying that my happiness is not dependent upon my husband's happiness, for instance, is simply not acknowledging reality. (Nor does it acknowledge those vows that make us one flesh.) Concern over money issues is a sure-fire guarantee that when one person is unhappy, others will be pulled along for the ride. *Especially* in a marriage!

Just consider average couple from Average Street. We will call them John and Jane...

> John and Jane collapse into bed. The air is stiff with the unhappiness that comes from unsettled discussion and problems. They both know they should not go to bed with anger or stress, and that makes them all the more tense. They lie there as stiff as the air, preparing for the fitful night ahead when neither one will sleep well.
>
> John and Jane are in a pickle. They feel trapped in the pit of debt. Every time they think they gain a foothold, they slip deeper. Knowing that the love of money is the root of many evils doesn't help John and Jane either, who toss and turn throughout the night in despair.
>
> (Chances are, if John and Jane took their eyes off their situation long enough to look around, they'd find that pit a) endless, and b) crowded with people just like them who are feeding off each other's misery.)

No one would walk around grinning and humming when a mate—or anyone in that person's family or circle of friends— is either suffering or dispirited. And has any of you ever danced with glee when someone close is on a rampage? Forget it!

We human beings are social creatures. Most of us live in some sort of community, whether in the home, at work, within the body of Christ, or through extended family. We gain strength when we remain in community with each other. Let's not forget the counsel of Romans 12:15: "Rejoice with those who rejoice; mourn with those who mourn." Our emotions are influenced by everyone around us and, to a lesser degree, by such variables as the weather, outcome of sporting events, and bad hair days.

Attitude, however, is one thing we can maintain, independent of any outside influence. Like joy, attitude isn't just an emotion. It is the underlying strength of character, spiritual maturity, and worldview from which emotions spring. It's the driveshaft of our emotional response. Our headwater, if you will. And we do have control over our attitude.

How we view the things we possess, how we view our work, and how we spend our free time all become a part of us and define who we are. This is all manifested through our attitude.

Can you have a half-glass-full attitude and still bawl your eyes out from time to time? Or clutch the steering wheel on your way to work until your knuckles turn white? Of course you can. But because your glass is half full, once you've vented your emotion, you will probably pick yourself up, dust yourself off, and face your next task with determined perseverance.

Would You...

- bend over to pick up a penny on the street?
- drive a dependable older vehicle?
- pick up lint or dirt from a floor or rug before it gets ground in?

Persevere

Keep reading in Romans 5. Paul begins to talk about character (which has a lot to do with attitude) and perseverance. Let me share what I have learned about perseverance.

A long time ago, I was in the insurance business. I was not a sales phenomenon, but I did learn one certain thing: Perseverance pays. If I persisted long enough, I would get the sale. I seldom failed.

I've applied the perseverance I learned in the business of insurance sales to the writing business. Sheer stick-to-itiveness has landed magazine articles and book contracts. Have I been so low that I was "finished with writing for good"? Yep. In times of such defeat and failure, "What's the use?" became my mantra. I wallowed in self-pity and staked a claim for every square inch of the mud puddle I was in. Yet I hung on, sometimes by grit, at least once because a friend would not let me quit.

Perseverance toward excellence in money skills is like that. It is also a way to overcome the selfish or unskilled behavior which seems to have become part of our American character. Let us never abandon our responsibility to develop and maintain our personal character, which so often is forged in hardship.

Smart Think:

Am I so afraid of failure that I don't risk change?

Trust in the Lord with All Your Heart

The Bible is crystal clear: Hardship is a normal part of this fallen world. Hardship does not always come from misfortune or others' misdeeds. Our attitude toward life can lead us to create our own hardship. Listen to Stuart Briscoe in *The Fruit of the Spirit:*

> Work and its significance and importance I understood. Service was a way of life I never questioned. Being weary with well-doing appeared to be the normal condition of those who lived in our house, and that was about it...It came as something of a shock to realize that perhaps my concept of the separated life had separated me from enrichment and unto impoverishment.

Can it be that even the best intentions interfere with good and proper stewardship of our lives, time, and money? You bet they can! Especially if you are a "doer."

I rank high among the doers in this world. I am the type that often fails to trust the Lord and really lean on Him. It is not so much a matter of wresting control of our lives from the Lord as it is a doer's constant push. Doers usually consider themselves obedient, read the Word, and *barge*. They are heave-ho personalities and get-things-done people. That translates to their Christian walk as well.

You want a doer to knit a tent, paint the house, bake bread for the month, and balance the checkbook by ten tonight? Okay.

You want a doer to write a book, feed the hungry, and save souls for Christ by noon tomorrow? Okay.

Doers tend to lean on themselves and forget how God provides for them on a daily basis. Not out of arrogance, mind you, but from the accustomed routine of getting things done. Yet the Lord says, "Trust Me, lean on Me. Don't forget that I am Lord of all, including your troubles and worries."

> God cannot endure that unfestive, mirthless attitude of ours in which we eat our bread in sorrow, with pretentious, busy haste, or even with shame. Through our daily meals He is calling us to rejoice, to keep holiday in the midst of our working day.
>
> —DIETRICH BONHOEFFER

Psalm 62

Listen to the bold cry of David: "Trust in him at all times, O people; pour out your hearts to him, for God is our refuge." When we pray Psalm 62, we put our trust in God alone. Yet so many of us put our trust elsewhere. Sure, if asked the question, we would confess our trust in God. In reality? Maybe if we invest in the market, maybe if we work overtime, maybe if we refinance the house, maybe if we try harder, do more...maybe if we bought a book!

All those things are good and right. But the source of our providence, the source of our hope, the source of our rest, the source of our riches is God alone. We must never forget that.

The story of a wealthy man goes like this:

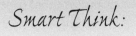

Smart Think:

I would rather put my eternal hope in
- all of my assets
- all of my intelligence and savvy
- God alone

Knowing he was going to die, a rich man pleaded with God to let him convert all of his assets into gold bars and bring them with him to heaven. At the Pearly Gates, Peter instructed the man to leave his possessions behind. "Oh, no," protested the rich man, "I have permission to bring my bars of gold." Exasperated, Peter called the Lord: "A fellow is here who claims You gave him permission to bring along his sack of gold bars, but for the life of me, I can't understand why he would want to bring *pavement!*"

Anchor your heart in God.
Count your blessings.
Give thanks.
Proceed.

The Adventures of Frugal Woman

The apostle Paul warned Timothy that the love of money is a root of many evils. That verse could never apply to me! Or so I thought. I regarded those as words for people who had money but wanted more, for the skinflint who hoarded his loot, or for the person obsessed with making the first million. Nope, clearly no application to my life!

Then one day, long ago, the Lord brought me up short. I had groused for weeks about a sudden change in our property tax assessment. "Woe is me" was my chant. "How will we ever manage? This tax is unfair..." He gently spoke to my spirit and reminded me of a few things. An actual conversation might sound like this: "Daughter, have I not always taken care of you? Why do you mock Me so by wringing your hands and whining all over town! Your focus is a little off these days; look back to Me."

～　～　～

Worry About Today

"Where are all the things I used to worry about? I don't even remember what they were."

My mother said that. We were in the car, headed to town, when she blurted that out. Maybe Mom's comment is all the sloganeering we need for one book. At 86, she's seen a lot of heartache, lived through hard times aplenty, and had her share of worry. Yet listen to what she said: *I don't even remember what those worries were.* Well, *I* can tell you: My mother's life was nothing but struggle. She raised three girls on waitress tips, worked long hours to get two of them through college, and lived with the bitter pain of an unfaithful spouse. That's just the big stuff. Yet where is her worry now? Mom would have to think hard to remember.

Sometimes worry becomes obsession and our money crunch keeps us pinned down, away from the liberating arms of God. Does that ever happen to you? Ask yourself some questions:

■ Does my worry over finances absorb my thoughts?

■ Do I consider myself orphaned by God because things are not going as well as I would like financially? Have I pulled myself out of His reach?

■ What do my bitter complaints say about my trust in the faithfulness and providence of my Father?

■ The Bible says, "Thou shalt not covet." Do I covet things, security, financial stability?

We all stand guilty of these sins, don't we? How well He knows our human frailties! That is why He gave us His written Word to guide us and His living Word, His Son, to lead us. "Do not worry," Jesus says to us. "Tomorrow will worry about itself (see Matthew 6:25-34). And just as Jesus taught us to pray, "Give us this day our daily bread," so it is that if we ask, seek, and knock, it will be given to us within His perfect will.

Consider the words of an inscription over an ancient mantelpiece in England:

> Fear knocked at the door. Faith answered. No one was there.

Jesus said to worry only about today. Can't get better advice than that! If I may, I will add this: Worry about today, and plan loosely for tomorrow. Here is what I have learned:

1. Today happens in spite of our worry.

2. Yesterday's plan helped today happen well.

3. We are content when today happens well.

> True contentment is a real, even an active virtue—not only affirmative but creative. It is the power of getting out of any situation all there is in it.
>
> —G.K. CHESTERTON

To Be Content

That's part of my creed...to be content, whatever state I am in. As evidenced by my story about the couch, sometimes I don't manage this virtue very well. Yet I can distinguish my superficial discontent toward outward matters—such as improvement of home decor, a better meatloaf, or losing a little weight—from deeper discontent. The "contentment" of the creed goes deeper; it goes to a place called inner peace.

For years we had a sign pasted on a mirror in our home that read, Draw a circle around yourself and be content with the space you are in. Try that for yourself, right now, and fasten your seat belt. We're embarking on our trip *toward* Easy Street now, and there are several stops along the way. First stop is...well, living within your means.

Attitude Adjustments

- Accomplish at least one thing that boosts your self-confidence today. If you are sick, that accomplishment might be walking to the bathroom to wash your face.

- Laugh and dance at least once each day.

- Be kind at least once each day—to others or to animal companions. Write a complimentary note to a friend, a service person, your mate.

- Celebrate creation. Walk in nature as on a pilgrimage. Give thanks for the bounty of all His works.

- Plan as best you can for the future; worry only about today.

- Live each day just to the extent of your ability.

- Push yourself a little to get more out of the day.

CHAPTER 3

Live Within Your Means

The American Dream

Not too long ago, the American dream was to own a home, to own a new car, and to send the kids to college. Know what it is today? To get out of debt. Yet at the same time we are struggling to get out of debt and to live within our means, the world tells us to spend. So spend we do. We spend to relieve tension, to escape, and to reward ourselves.

Today, nearly 110 million Americans have 950 million credit cards—almost nine cards per person. The average person buys thousands of dollars of products and services each year with those credit cards and has an outstanding balance to match. During the Christmas season we will pull out VISA alone over 200 million times—about 5500 times each minute. That does not include any of the other 2000 cards available. Statistically, putting a credit card in someone's hand means a 34 percent greater purchase overall. (Harry S. Dahlstrom, *Out of Hock* [Holliston, MA: Dahlstrom and Company, Incorporated, 1994].)

> **Smart Think:**
>
> Spend money as you may, but you can only spend it once!

The American Nightmare

"I have more outgo than I do income," we say with a chuckle, and others chuckle along because they share the same

41

sentiment and circumstance. Though our words resonate, we fool ourselves into thinking we have no trouble managing finances because we are able to pay our monthly bills. "Able to afford," has come to mean "able to afford *payments*." Many of us are one or two paychecks away from hunger or homelessness.

Who doesn't resent this state of affairs? *USA Today* says money is the number one cause of arguments in the family and recently reported that only 28 percent of parents polled feel they have taught good money habits to their children. In all of my talks and travels, I have yet to meet one person who had never felt chagrined about financial flubs.

People want the burden of money woes lifted. They want to cushion the future—to at least be prepared for the emergency car repair or for Missy's braces. They want an empty bill file and a full wallet. Many would like to use their money for the aid and nourishment of those less fortunate. And nearly everyone wishes for greater skill and discipline with savings.

The Adventures of Frugal Woman

Here are two stories that should pose as a wake-up call for anyone under the age of 50!

Gladys isn't her name, of course, but a name I've given this lovely saint. Gladys attended a women's retreat I spoke at years ago. Her story, and that of another woman, still causes me to shake my head in sorrow.

I introduced a simple exercise. "Write one word that describes how you feel about your financial circumstance." "Blessed," said one. "Guilty," said another. "Frustrated," said another. And then we came to Gladys, the charming grandma in the group, the church lady supreme. Gladys was probably the pillar of her church, the one who knit mittens for the poor, who made fabulous casseroles for potlucks, and who hunkered down on her prayer bones to pray for your very soul. Gladys said she was *scared*.

What have I gotten into, I worried to myself as every head in the room whipped to attention and utter silence prevailed. Gladys chose to continue speaking.

"I can't live with this burden any longer," she said. "I have to let it out. You see, my husband's retirement isn't enough for us to get along on, and every month I go to the bank and borrow more money on our credit cards."

The gasp in the room was audible. Yet as sorrowful as her declaration was, I've run into many a Gladys over the years. My second story is of an elderly widow at another retreat. This lady was filled with dignity and bore herself with a warm but confident manner. If ever a woman "had it all together," she did! Frankly, I wondered why she even bothered to attend a retreat on money management. Yet when I challenged the women in the church to write a paragraph describing their financial predicament, that woman put her head in her hands and wept bitter tears.

Not a Second to Lose

I don't know what happened to Gladys or that elegant widow. (Women in Gladys' church assured me that they would find a way to help.) From time to time I think of them—and so many like them—and offer a prayer of supplication on their behalf. On *your* behalf, let me entreat you to learn a lesson from these two dear women. Live within your means now to lessen the chance of weeping one day yourself. The stark reality about

Smart Think:

Can't afford something? Then how can you afford the full price of that thing *plus* interest?

money problems, indebtedness, or mismanagement is that every *second* that ticks by adds up to more cost to you. Usually in the form of interest. If you are committed to learning some skills to help alleviate your financial woes, you don't have a minute to spare.

Committed? Ready, Set, Go!

It should be simple, shouldn't it? Just spend less than you take in. *Hah*, you say. *If I could do that, I wouldn't be holding your book in my hands. Never mind the American dream...my life is more like* Nightmare on Elm Street! *It's* not *simple. Once and for all, I need to learn what to do so I can finally figure out how to live within my means. Know what I mean?* Yes, I do. And I am certain that if you cultivate a positive attitude and practice the skills presented in this book, you will at least be able to sleep more soundly without those pesky nightmares going bump in the night.

These first few chapters have been (as my mother would say) all talk and no action. We are about to turn a corner and get to work. (A spiral notebook would be mighty handy.) Let's start with some frank questions.

- What do your financial problems do to you emotionally?

- How well do you think your present financial priorities line up with the Bible?

- What are you most likely to buy on impulse? What would your mate buy? What would your children buy?

- What would you like your children or grandchildren to remember about the way you handle money?

If you are sincere about wanting to manage on the income you now have, you can't just blast off into the sunset armed with nothing but a new outlook. You need a strong launching pad. That launching pad is called a plan.

Plan for Success

If you've bought any of the following, raise your hand:

- a computer program to help you manage finances successfully

- books to help you manage finances successfully

- a special tablet filled with lines and categories to help you set up a budget to help manage finances successfully

Chances are you bought one of those tools to help you manage finances, to keep good records, and to stay on top and in control. Chances also are that you began with a bang but abandoned your resolve to stay on top as soon as life got in the way. So how *are* you doing in the discipline department? For most of you, I know the answer: *ack!* (That is why so much emphasis in the previous chapter is on recommitment.) For some reason, even though we recognize the importance of planning and maintaining good money management, we run into a real disconnect with our behavior. That reason, I believe, is simple human nature.

We tend to procrastinate, partly because we keep expecting our finances to improve enough to give us a fresh start on any plan, budget, or management strategy. Also, many of us avoid anything that is unpleasant or difficult; few of us avoid things that are pleasant or easy. But think about this: By putting off the thing we don't like to do, we add guilt and anxiety to the drudgery of it all!

How Do You Feel?

Suppose an on-the-street reporter stuck a mike in your face on your way out of MoreBargainsGalore and asked if you felt comfortable with your financial future. What would you say? If your answer was "Yeah, for the most part," think again. Look

Smart Think:

In uncertain times, go back to the basics.

to see where most of your money goes in a given month. Is the bulk of your income immediately consumed? Does it fly out the door to pay bills? Those in the know say fully one-fourth of us save nothing toward our financial future. No plan equals no safety net; no plan equals no future.

B...B...Budget

Would this be a bona fide book on money management if it didn't bring up that horrid word? Here goes—another word for plan is *budget*. Have you ever tried to budget, or do you just face each paycheck with a shrug and think, *What bills do I have to pay this month?* You may not want to go so far as accounting for every single expenditure, but you cannot begin to live within your means unless you know what your "means" are. The use and habit of a sensible budget will reveal your "means" to you, in black and white, once and for all ending all speculation or presumption. It will also liberate you to spend wisely, to prepare for your future, and to feel ready for whatever may come your way.

Don't be intimidated by the word "budget"! As I wrote in my book *Money & Me,* a budget is like meatloaf. Meatloaf requires certain ingredients; what you add to the basics depends on your recipe. And every cook has his or her own concoction.

Budgets are like that. You have certain fixed expenses that must be paid. And then there are extra expenses that make your budget unique to you. Your budget is your recipe, and it can be as homemade or as store-bought as you like.

In your budget, you set limits and prioritize. This is not, as they say, rocket science, but elementary and sensible: *A budget is how much you plan in advance to spend.*

That is not intimidating, it's empowering!

Getting on Track

Honest effort goes into setting a budget. Though I give you basic skills here, you may want to visit the library (or dust off one of those budget books on your bookshelf).

First, you track. "Tracking" is an age-old method used to reveal and evaluate spending habits and patterns. Begin by listing your fixed monthly expenses. Your checkbook register will help immensely. (By the way, your checkbook register says a lot about how you live your life.) These are the payments that stay pretty much the same from month to month. Here is a list that can help you get started:

■ mortgage

■ car payments

■ utilities (including telephone and garbage)

■ insurance

■ taxes

■ charitable contributions

■ debt payments

■ savings and investments

Now try your best to track your unfixed expenses. These are the ones that vary from month to month. Unless you live in a home you realistically cannot afford, or you are doling out car payments on an ego trip you are foolish to drive, I am convinced this rather unregulated area of money management is where we end up in trouble.

■ food

■ clothing (new purchases, laundry, and dry-cleaning)

■ other housing costs (home maintenance and repairs, furniture, utilities)

■ other transportation costs (gas, auto maintenance and repairs, tolls, parking)

- medical expense

- children's expenses (including education, allowance, clubs, and other activities)

- personal gifts

- restaurants and entertainment (and baby-sitting)

- personal improvement

- recreation, vacation, and travel

- pets

- newspaper and magazines

- walking-around money

Now prioritize. I believe we set ourselves up for failure if we do not tailor our spending and saving plan. Take a good long look at what you've tracked. Where do you overspend? Where can you cut back? Where can you sacrifice? Where do you refuse to sacrifice? In our home, we simply refuse to sacrifice when it comes to organic food, olive oil in particular. Yes, organic is more expensive, but I have enough consumer savvy to stay within a remarkably low monthly food allowance and still buy extra-virgin, cold-press oil.

Look at your expense-tracking record. Put a smile next to the expenditures that are important to you or to your family. Now look at all the other entries. Would the world stop spinning if you didn't have an espresso every morning? Would a romp in the leaves and a walk around the neighborhood (or other creative cost-free recreation) do instead of a costly trip to the movies? Put a frown next to expenses that can be reduced or eliminated.

Now, the In Box. Once you know how much you spend, you need to look at how much you earn. Summarize all of your income from every source.

Ready, set, budge! Design your budget.

Having trouble budging? Maybe a little advice from the Lord will help:

> Go to the ant, you sluggard;
>> consider its ways and be wise!
> It has no commander,
>> no overseer or ruler,
> yet it stores its provisions in summer
>> and gathers its food at harvest.
> How long will you lie there, you sluggard?
>> When will you get up from your sleep?
> A little sleep, a little slumber,
>> a little folding of the hands to rest—
> and poverty will come on you like a bandit
>> and scarcity like an armed man (Proverbs 6:6-11).

And if Others Won't Budge?

You may live in a family or share your home with others who balk at any suggestion of money management or any talk of living within your means. Others may take this notion as an insult, punishment, or a threat. This can be a frustrating roadblock to your effort and intent. So let's talk about others.

Since men who are reckless (or manipulative) with money are statistically a greater threat to financial security than women (sorry guys, that's what the experts claim), I will deal here with a stubborn husband in particular. Needless to say, these same principles may be applied to any adult, regardless of gender.

Husbands

In their book *Money Demons,* Susan Forward and Craig Buck are straightforward: Women, they say, usually *know* when they are out of control or mismanaging funds. Men, on the other hand, rarely own up to wrong behavior and even more rarely will try to do anything about it.

If you are dealing with such a man, you are in a huge dilemma. You may feel trapped, afraid, or angry. You may even

feel like a hero, taking charge, controlling all the money trans-
actions, setting a budget...and bailing him out. Again.

What do you do? First, pray earnestly. Then...

1. *Get to the root of the problem.* This may mean con-
   vincing him to meet with counselors who can discuss
   his spending patterns and determine if there are underlying sins or internal factors involved.

2. *Set limits.* Be prepared for some fallout when spending
   limits are established. If you lay down the law, so to
   speak, you may have some rough sledding ahead
   because he may challenge or defy any parameters.

3. *Make him accountable.* A trusted friend, a pastor, or a
   financial counselor can become a very important team
   player right now.

4. *Ask him to pay the bills.* If he is irresponsible with funds
   now, this could be dangerous. In the right circumstance, however, dispersing the monthly "outgo" may
   be the wake-up call he needs. He won't find a snooze
   button on *this* alarm!

Children

Should you involve children in your effort to live within
your means? By all means!

The Bible tells us in Proverbs 22:6 to train children in the
way they should go, and when they are old they will not turn
from it. You are the one who can best teach your child thrift
and sound money management. How do you do that? By
example.

Frankly, this might be a good time to address the needs,
wants, and desires of that insatiable little consumer of yours.
Here are some suggestions:

1. *Mute the TV commercials.* If you, an adult, can be
   seduced into buying a product because of its dramatic
   claims and punchy jingle, imagine how a child's mind

is affected. This is a worrisome predicament. Just think of the phenomenally high cost of toy sets that accompany children's motion pictures!

2. *Set limits when your kids are in the cradle.* We naturally want to buy every cute baby outfit and gadget that MoreBargainsGalore has to offer. But giving in to such a desire can be your downfall—and your kids'. You, not your child, are the one getting the thrill from him or her looking like a model for Madison Avenue. Give your children messages right from the beginning; teach them a simple, godly life. That is abundance enough. (Leave the armloads of gifts to the grandparents. I, a grandmother of two, have budgeted for this thrill and am ever ready to step up to the plate.)

3. *Talk to your children about financial decisions in their language as soon as they can comprehend.* "We don't do that" or "No way, José" just won't do. Kids live in a social world, too, and they are pressured to fit in. Peer pressure is a big issue for children, especially adolescents and teens. Simply crossing your arms and slamming your foot down might only create hurt and rebellion in your kids.

4. *Define financial parameters to the children.* Without scaring them, assemble bills and a notepad. Convene a family meeting when no one is hurried. The purpose of the meeting is to show the kids your income and outgo. Use dollar bills and coins—or beans—to illustrate. At all times, assure them that you are responsible for the family's stewardship, you have a handle on things, and they should not worry.

Ask your children what they think they could do to cut back or to save, both individually and corporately. Provide incentive for good behavior, such as a "recreation" jar or "vacation" jar to collect savings.

5. *Don't deny your kids everything.* Nothing is wrong with treating your child to a special treat once in a while.

Others

Statistics say you are likely to spend more money when shopping with a friend. And while we may be able to resist the gushing enthusiasm and encouragement from a friend to buy that new outfit, what happens when a restaurant check lands on the table at Ribs "R" Us? You may want to participate in a meal with friends when you are severely limited financially. What happens when you are asked to split the cost of a meal equally after you've skipped the beverage and dessert and ordered frugally to boot?

1. Try to arrange for separate checks from the start.

2. Try to announce from the start that you would like to go Dutch treat.

3. Explain to your friends that you really want to share the cost with them, but your budget is limited and you'd rather pay for the part of the check that is actually yours. (This may only work with close friends who will be sensitive to your request and not interpret it as an appeal to a free meal.)

4. Don't forget to tip good service.

This book is crammed with my method, with proven guidelines, and with countless tips that will make life on one income a bit less daunting and a whole lot more possible. I want to share three ideas with you now—three principles that will give you immediate success, which is something we all need when we're turning over a new leaf. The principles are these: Simply skip, mandate moratorium, and sayonara impulse.

Simply Skip

This is such an easy principle! Skip a day, skip a week. You pick. Just avoid spending money on one thing that you can do without every other day or week. Here are a few examples:

- Suppose you routinely buy an espresso drink every weekday. Let's say your daily output is $3. Bring coffee from home or tote a water jug and skip your purchase every other day. By skipping two days each week, you save $6, or $24 each month, or $288 each year. By skipping three days each week, the savings are: $9, $36, and $432. Cold turkey gets you $15, $60, and $720. (This does not factor in the impulse muffin or the tip jar.) Do you have a pressing bill that $720 could pay right now? And that is just from espresso! If skipping is really, really hard, buy tea or coffee-to-go for one-third the price of espresso.

> Drinking water can actually help reduce fat deposits. When you are fully hydrated, your body is better able to transport fat to the muscles for burning. Pass up that next latte, drink a glass of water, and keep the fat in your wallet.

- Suppose you routinely go to the movies. Skip a weekend and watch videos from your collection in the bookcase. Or watch *Saturday Night Cinema* on PBS. Or borrow a video from the library.

Try this: Buy the Friday paper and read every single page. Is the high school playing basketball on Saturday? Is the Methodist church sponsoring a potluck? Can you square dance at the Fraternal Order of Grizzly Bears? Is the college offering a free course or lecture? Are a bunch of five-year-olds having a dance recital? Who cares if you know anyone...have some free fun!

Outdoor Family Fun

- Stay up very late and learn about the stars. You can get a guidebook from the library.

- Get up *very* early, make a thermos of hot cider or mint tea, and go as a family to a nearby lake, lock, ocean, river, stream, reservoir, pond, or puddle. Sit and sip tea and watch the world awaken. Please try to do this one. You will help create a memory your children will cherish.

- Establish a holiday tradition (that seems to the children to show you've lost your mind). Have ice-cream sundaes for dinner and then take an evening ride to gawk at Christmas lights. While you are out, find a diner and swivel on counter stools while you drink hot chocolate.

- Organize a neighborhood summer Olympics with a twist: Ask everyone to bring and include their animal companions. Seeing the new version of the three-legged race is worth the effort!

- Go for a hike in a new neighborhood. Look for ideas to take home: interesting paint combinations, gardens, landscaping, mailboxes. Joseph and I are incurable explorers. We often venture into an unexplored part of town to cruise or walk the streets.

- Paint your mailbox. Make it fun. Put everyone's name on the outside.

- Rainy day fun: Get enough copies of a certain play (Shakespeare, maybe?) from a library for all the family members. Then act out the play, reading from the script.

- Once and for all—go to that museum or art gallery in your town. Get dressed up before you go.

- Show up at a hospital or nursing home and ask if there is anything you can do to help.

Skip a Visit to the Grocery Store!

What?! Sure! Here's what I mean:

Many of us have developed a routine and shop at a certain time every single week. We may go on Wednesday morning after the supermarket ads hit the paper, Saturday afternoon when the kids stay home with dad, or Friday night on the way home from work. The routine is automatic, and old habits die hard. After all, isn't this what our mothers did? Yes, but much of what our mothers bought was fresh and had a short shelf life, so they had to shop routinely. Thanks to modern chemistry, chances are you have cereal in your pantry that has been languishing for months. *Ick!* Use it up or feed that stuff to the compost! (Notice I did not say "throw that stuff out.")

Ask yourself, *Have I turned shopping into routine?*

Pledge not to be dazzled by the latest sale—sales will always be with us! See if you can skip your usual date with the mega-mart. Send someone else to the store with just enough money for the milk, bread, eggs, or anything else you absolutely, positively must have during this period. As a bonus,

1. You can use the time you normally spend shopping on something else—like organizing your world.

2. You will feel resourceful.

3. Your children will not grow up thinking they have to shop every week. Or have a latte every day.

The Adventures of Frugal Woman

It could only happen to me: death by potato peel. And all because we were on a moratorium...

From time to time, Wonder Man and I go on a complete spending moratorium. It may last days or weeks.

I believe we were in our third week when I poisoned myself.

Ever notice how potatoes suddenly harken back to their Irish roots and turn green? Mine got so green I expected to hear bagpipes belting out "Danny Boy." But I couldn't let them go to waste, so I ate them. All of them. Before you could say "Erin go braugh," I was on the phone with poison control in Atlanta.

"Pardon me," I croaked, "but I seem to have consumed several green potatoes, fully clad I might add. My body feels like ten miles of really bad country road."

Imagine my surprise to learn that potatoes contain a natural toxin called solanine, a nerve poison. And where, might I ask, is this solanine found? In the green—which I was at that very moment.

〜 〜 〜

Just Say Whoa...the Mandated Moratorium

Want to live within your means? Don't shop. Period. Or at least don't shop for a period.

It has long intrigued me that people shop for recreation. Nothing drives this home more than when I travel and land in a fabulous destination, replete with activity and stunning natural wonder, to see hoards of people with fanny packs weaving in and out of stores filled with the usual tourist stuff. We need to connect the dots here: What do people usually do when they go into a store? Why, they shop. Bingo! Am I saying *never* shop for fun? No. That would be fanatical. (Do I shop for fun? In a deliberate sense, yes. Joseph and I enjoy a little antiquing now and again, always on the alert for an old tea tin to add to our collection.) All I'm encouraging us to do is give it a rest, go sit on a beach, or climb a mountain and yodel.

We have practiced the principle of moratorium in our home for so long that it has become an anticipated and positive experience. We do not spend money (other than on bills) within the prescribed period, be it a week or more. At times we've declared moratoriums because of financial red alert. At other times, we simply knew the time had come to use accumulated goods on hand, be they food or even books that needed reading. Our time-tested principle of using things up really struts its stuff during our moratoriums. We have entertained others while on moratorium, sent fabulous gifts while on moratorium, and eaten some of our most memorable meals using our creative genius (much more on that later) while on moratorium. Why, during one moratorium, I even learned the importance of storing potatoes in a cool, *dark* place.

> *Smart Think:*
>
> Should it be fun to shop? Yes!
> Should you shop for fun? No!
> (Okay, okay...once in a while.)

Some of you are no strangers to moratoriums—they have been forced on you by dwindling income. You are intimately acquainted with this mandate and couldn't spend a quarter on chewing gum right now. Or maybe you don't like where this is heading...after all, a person should have some rewards and pleasures in life, right? Of course, right! Yet if you want to manage on what you have, you have to give and take...right?

Remember all that talk about right attitude in the previous chapter? Just turn your latest spending standstill into adventure and call it a positive exercise in money management or a deliberate, mandated moratorium. Because it is.

(Moratoriums, of course, do not apply to necessary expenditures that may affect our safety, health, well-being, or that of others.)

Sayonara, Impulse!

Experts claim that 50 percent of what we buy, we buy on impulse, and 25 percent of what we buy, we don't need at all. Retailers spend hundreds of thousands of dollars to learn how to beguile us and to convince us "we gotta have." *Do not do it.*

Do not buy on impulse. Use a list when you shop for groceries. Put on blinders when looking for a specific piece of clothing. Be careful. Ask yourself if you really need an item. Drive it around in your cart and think. Chances are you can live without it. And live within your means. Here's an issue I will talk about later: Much of what we buy is bought because we felt we would use, eat, or wear the thing. Where is it now? We might be alarmed to see how much clutter we've accumulated—from retail, wholesale, or even bargain thrift stores—that *just occupies space.*

Statisticians inform grocers that every time you walk through their wide automatic doors and grab a cart, you will buy more than you planned. Few and far between are the disciplined souls who can walk in, buy only what they want, and walk out again. Near the entrance (where you'd practically trip over them) and strung all along your route are the latest "sales" the market wants you to spring for. They are irresistible.

Do I buy on impulse? You might call it "planned impulse." Do I shop for the sake of shopping? Sure I do—but not *ever* from boredom or routine, and rarely to amuse myself. I have learned how to isolate the best buy in an entire store in no time—and to quickly determine need, want, or desire. If this were an Olympic event, I'd bring home the gold. You can, too, by being smart.

A good way to avoid impulse buying is to think down the road:

■ Will this new gizmo-gadget really be used after the first flurry of entertainment or novelty is over?

■ Will I wear this (or fit into it) in a couple of months? Next year? (Do fashions last into next *year?* They do if you go with a classic look and update accessories.)

■ Will I really use this sauce, or do I just want another pretty jar in my kitchen cupboard? (By the way, I sometimes opt for the pretty jar. And those tea tins? Filled

with herbal, green, and black teas for our sipping pleasure.)

> Next time you think you can't live without an appli-
> ance (espresso machine, juicer, soft ice cream dis-
> penser, bread machine, pasta machine...), *borrow* one
> first. Bet you have a friend who has one in the cup-
> board...or garage. If you use it—especially after you
> learn how much work goes into using it and cleaning
> it—begin to look for the best deal you can find. Maybe
> your friend would be delighted to sell you hers.

The Adventures of Frugal Woman

Let me share two "planned impulse" moments, one
that happened at a big-box discounter in Reno, Nevada,
another that will happen some day in the future:

1. I am fond of Chai (tea) latte. Chai latte is a pretty
    spendy proposition in the real world. So I make
    it myself. I've gathered the ingredients and
    learned the protocol for making a good Chai. But
    to make a fabulous Chai, I needed a handheld
    frother.

    I needed to educate myself: How much
    should a frother cost? How much should a frother
    on sale cost? Once I figured this out, I began the
    search. It wasn't an outright mission, just the
    tucking of the frother idea in the back of my
    mind. Months later (I didn't die for want of a
    frother during this time), while checking the
    clearance rack at a store in Reno, there it was...at
    half the amount I'd expected to pay on sale.
    Sudden impulse? Nope. Planned impulse.

2. I need two off-white, quilted pillow shams for our guest room. Someday I will find them at such a screaming deal I will plop my shekels down immediately and leave some store grinning. Does our guest room look okay now, without this final touch? Sure it does. Will it look even better when I find and "impulsively" buy the shams? Yep. I'll wait.

~   ~   ~

> Better one handful with tranquility than two handfuls with toil and chasing after the wind.
>
> —ECCLESIASTES 4:6

Practical Matters Matter

Living Well on One Income is about to shift from a *philosophical* thrust to the *practical* aspects of my system.

Keeping the creed in mind—particularly the part about using our possessions wisely—the next chapter points out that in order to use things we first have to be able to *find* them!

CHAPTER 4

Let's Organize!

A sign hangs at my husband's workplace: "A clean desk is the mark of a sick mind." The sign hangs as a humorous apologetic for any "desk mess" in the area. Wry smiles and chuckles abound as the virtue of a fastidious or industrious person suffers good-natured ridicule. While I chuckle along with others at the impertinence of that message, I *can* tell you what a clean desk *is* a mark of: someone with a greater chance than most at successfully managing finances. An ordered life is a smart and frugal life.

We may joke about the "neatnicks" among us, but I'm guessing there are more from their ranks who laugh all the way to the bank, than from those who live in clutter. While organization and tidiness are sometimes carried to extremes, these virtues go a long way toward sound financial management. Why? At least one organization expert claims that nearly 20 percent of a cluttered person's budget goes to crisis purchases because of that clutter. This same person maintains that the average American spends up to one hour each day looking for misplaced items. One hour each day, she says, equals six lost weeks each year. Lost! As lost as your wallet, your eyeglasses, your library card, the bill that must be paid, the pliers...

Whoa! Now I Gotta Clean My Living Room to Save Money?!

In a sense, yes. Once again, I am not talking about being a fanatic. I never intend to encourage fanatic behavior in anything, whether a philosophical point or a practical suggestion. But consider the logic here.

A clean desk, if I may take license with that plaque in Joe's office, is a mark of someone who...

■ takes pride in appearance

■ is a good steward

■ does not have to replace hard-to-locate items

■ does not waste time looking for things

■ feels happier because of pleasant surroundings

■ uses things for which money was paid

Clean Desk Dude

Let's "organize" the characteristics of a clean-desk dude and explore each one to learn all we can from this principle.

Takes pride. I am convinced that the outer person is usually a good indicator of the inner person. When someone is kind, altruistic, and gentle, we say that person has...what? A good hairdo? No. We say that person has a good heart. I believe that an ordered, peaceful exterior can be a good indicator of an ordered, peaceful inside.

Is a good steward. Let's look at tidiness and cleanliness as vital factors of good stewardship. I have seen homes with so much clutter that whatever is laying at the bottom of the heap on the floor, stuck in the closet, left on the dresser, or hidden in the garage is hopelessly lost.

Clutter needn't be as dramatic as a pile on the floor. Think about the clothes in your dresser or closet. Think about your coats and jackets alone! Who is the better steward—the person who gives unused coats and clothes to cover the naked, or those who possessively cling to their mohair *just because?* It might fit again, it might come back into fashion, it once was a favorite coat, it originally cost a fortune...these all fit in the category of *just because.*

Stewardship is not just about giving; it is about care. Look at it this way: Every single thing you have owned, now own, and will own is a gift from God. It is part of His providence. We slap Him in the face when we fail to care for that which He has entrusted to us.

Will not duplicate items. When you are organized, you know what you have. And when you know what you have, you will not duplicate what you have. Time for a new adventure.

The Adventures of Wonder Man

Joseph must have dozens of pliers. (I may be exaggerating, but not much.) He must have at least one of every tool invented by man, starting with the first wheel. Many of these tools were bequeathed in one way or another. But the pliers are a problem.

Just why does he have so many pliers? At one time, due to lack of space, the only place he could store his tools was in big, galvanized garbage pails. Those pesky pliers always seemed to get lost in those pails. And every time Joseph needed pliers, off to the store he went. Which is why he now has dozens of pliers.

~ ~ ~

Does not waste time. Time and money are surely the most fleeting things in life. They can also be squandered. Time can be squandered in a more insidious way than money.

Experts teach us how to manage our time more effectively. One area in need of improvement is the time we spend looking for things. (I spend an average of ten minutes each day looking for my eyeglasses!)

In a well-organized home, just about everything has its own spot, its own place. Anyone who needs something simply goes to the spot where it "lives." This principle does double duty because it helps allay the problem of clutter in your home, shop, or workplace. Here is what I mean...

For the record, I resent being called a neat-freak. I am simply organized, most especially in my kitchen. I don't draw pictures in my cupboards and insist that dishes and pots and pans go back to their outline, but as corny as this may sound, everything *does* have a place—or at least a general area—where it is stored.

One shelf in my kitchen holds a cluster of thick, white coffee mugs; on another our drinking glasses line up in neat corn rows; colorful platters bring life to a dull corner as they nest in a wooden dish rack; the salt grinder always returns to its own nest in a small brown crock. We never have a second thought where things go when emptying the dishwasher or clearing the table. Never any clutter, never any search, and never any waste of time. (Unless I'm looking for my eyeglasses.)

This needn't be crazed. You're going to empty the dishwasher anyway. Why not put everything in its own spot? This actually takes less energy than trying to jam *another* cup or glass into a cluttered cupboard. Speaking of *jamming*, if your coffee mugs have succeeded in cloning themselves and you risk a concussion each time you open the cupboard, bring the herd down to a manageable number. Put the excess mugs in your yard sale box.

Feels happier. Let's face it—you feel happier when your living space or work space is clean and ordered. An ordered life is very gratifying. Strive to make your home an oasis of serenity and peace. Directing attention to goals and aspirations is easier in a harmonious atmosphere. If you have young children, do the best you can without becoming some weird tyrant. Children can learn order. One organizational expert cites a kindergarten classroom as proof!

Those of you with older children may opt to follow the system we used when our own son was a young man. His room was his space, cluttered or clean, and we respected that. General household living areas, however, were kept neat (but "lived-in") by all.

Uses things. This is one of my favorite principles. I'll use an imaginary desk from Joe's workplace for this example. Let's build a messy desk: papers stacked in messy piles that cover everything, a coffee mug so moldy it's growing Portobello mushrooms, and dust. Under the piles of paper also rest a stapler, an assortment of quality ballpoints, a name plate, an expensive ink pen, a day planner that shows entries for the first two weeks of 1999, note pads, personalized stationery, books, family pictures, and, of course, a collection of the ubiquitous penny.

Every single item on that messy desk was purchased by someone at one time. With money. Seems to me it would make just as much sense to open a window and fling the money to the birds. At least they would put it to use building their own "nest egg."

Smart Think:

What is my desk a mark of?

Let's Organize Your World!

Organization is the rock on which we build success. We will discuss three distinct aspects of organization:

1. Organize every place you have a collection of *things*.

2. Make lists.

3. Find time.

Things

Organization of things can take Herculean or Lilliputian effort, but the process is all the same. You may need to organize an entire room or a tiny jewelry case. Where you start doesn't matter; beginning the process does. Living well does not depend upon *how* you organize, but it does mean *that* you organize.

Does organization ever end? Nope. It just gets easier. I go about my own organization systematically. Right now I have sights on my bathroom. I will most likely go the Lilliputian route and designate one tiny chore each day. I'll address the basket with hair gizmos one day, the basket of face cream the next, and the cluster of plants in the corner the next. I may hunker down and scour the clawfoot the next day, and so on.

What will I actually do? I will go through *everything,* find homes for things I do not or will not use, remind myself of things I've accumulated and make a mental note to use them, repot plants that have outgrown their containers, and change the look of the room by moving things around. For instance, I'm thinking about transferring my rolled white washcloths from the breadbasket they've been camped in for years into a blue-banded crock. I'm also thinking about putting a lace valance on a skinny window.

When I am finished with my bathroom, I will snake my way around the house, one room at a time, one drawer or shelf or closet at a time, until I've worked my way through the entire house. It might take me a year. I'm in no hurry. I'm always moving inventory, constantly finding opportunities to put more pizzazz into life by utilizing, enjoying, rerouting, or rearranging belongings.

How Do I Organize Thee? Let Me Count the Ways...

Where are the usual places that need organizing? We will look at what I consider the top ten in the "Clutter Hall of Fame." Let's start with numero uno...

1. Under the kitchen sink. Do you know what you have under there right now? Allow me: dried orange peel, dead coffee grounds, balled-up pieces of paper, enough empty jars to float the Queen Elizabeth II, enough products to clean the Empire State Building, enough plastic sacks to start your own grocery store, and an assortment of rusted Brillo pads.

2. The freezer. This one ties for first place. The freezer is like a cosmic black hole. We put things in there, never to be seen again. Do we ever think of putting on a pair of gloves and actually *inventorying* every freezer-burned hunk of jerky? Why, no! It's much too comforting to know the stuff is there, inedible though it is.

3. The medicine cabinet. I know, you're saving that unused antibiotic for your next toothache, the cough medicine from 1986 (which you will forget about, anyway, next time you're hacking away) for the flu season, and you have enough allergy medicine to keep a platoon of paratroopers from sneezing. Where did all that baby aspirin come from? And why are there rusting *pennies* in the medicine cabinet? Not to mention extra toothbrushes. (Coffee mugs, toothbrushes, and wire clothes hangers self-produce spontaneously. I have it on the best authority.)

4. The glove compartment. We keep everything *but* gloves in these places: paper napkins by the gross from fast-food joints, plastic spoons and forks, cassettes with tape hanging like loopy spaghetti, receipts by the bucketful... and pennies.

5. The refrigerator. This could look like a science project. I admit, this is *one* place where I am fanatic. Order in the fridge! The fridge door compartments deserve special mention—you *are* planning to serve salad to the

entire population of Delaware with all of that salad dressing, aren't you?

6. The Bills Paid file. Better watch out! You don't want to get caught without paid receipts for your electric bills from 1910. Or your car insurance policy that has renewed every six months since you bought that DeSoto.

7. The spice rack. You do know that these things lose their spicy and herby qualities within a year or two, don't you? (Much more on these in a later chapter.) But, hey! Never know when you are going to need a whopping quarter teaspoon of garam masala. And garlic powder! Mustn't get caught without, which explains the three separate jars.

8. The shop bench. Now where are those pliers?

9. The stuffed-toy hammock in the children's room. This has vexed me for years! I can't actually *see* the collection of stuffed animals—if it is, indeed, a collection. It's actually a pile of fur buried under the latest creature that was played with for a few hours and forgotten when the next furry creature came along, compliments of grandparents and friends, or as a healthy alternative to creaming Junior when he threw a fit in the toy section of MoreBargainsGalore.

10. The shoe rack. Or the lack thereof. This is a good place to organize. You never know, someone in the world just might be walking around barefoot.

Honorable mention goes to women's pocketbooks and kitchen junk drawers. No explanation needed.

Lists

If organization is the rock on which you build success, list making is the cornerstone of organization. With a list, you find that you *do* have time for things. But be careful! I, for one, am an inveterate list maker, but my lists used to look like this:

Monday

- repave driveway

- save rainforest

- bake seven dozen muffins and three trays of lasagna

- do quiet time, exercise, read *War and Peace*

A finger-wagging from Joseph cautioned me that I was becoming a slave to my lists and spending so much time planning that I missed the moment. I am rehabilitated now and try to limit my expectations.

List making, however, can be invaluable in your quest toward sound money management. Lists help you gain control of the day—help you seize the day. Lists can help you maintain your balance. They are invaluable in stewardship of time and money.

> We plan—and God steps in with another plan for us and He is all-wise and the most loving friend we have, aways helping us.
>
> —Nettie Fowler McCormick

A List of Lists

1. A list of what you plan to buy—especially at the supermarket. Also, a list on which to note things that need replacing. When you use the last of something, immediately walk to your "To Get" list and write it down. Why is this important? Let's say you use the last of your

garlic powder, but you did not write it on your list. Now, say, you have company coming to dinner and absolutely, positively *must* have garlic powder for your splendid Italian recipe. Stress. Hurry. Emergency trip to the store—the closest and perhaps the most expensive store. Who cares—just get it! Get it?

2. An annual list (on a calendar delegated for this use only) of birthdays, anniversaries, and graduations. We actually keep a binder with a record of gifts given. Do we always remember to write in this binder? Nope, but we try.

3. Annual lists of maintenance projects for your home and car. You do know you should fertilize your lawn every fall, right?

4. Annual and monthly lists of projects you hope to accomplish.

5. Daily lists that include phone calls, necessary paperwork, household chores, minimum and maximum projects and work to accomplish, items to purchase, and appointments.

6. A list of everything that must be done that day away from home and the route that will save you the most time and gas.

7. A list of upcoming events, especially when children are in the home.

Record Keeping

If you get into the habit of list making and want to be extra efficient, you might make records for yourself and for your heirs. Such records might include information about your banking, insurance, medical condition, investments, retirement, real estate, and vehicles.

I make a photocopy "collage" of all my important wallet stuff: driver's license, health insurance card, credit or bank cards, library card, and donor card. I give one copy to my mom and keep one in my sock drawer or suitcase. If I lose my wallet, I will save time, money, and anxiety by knowing exactly what I have lost.

List-Making Rules

1. Don't become a slave to your list. (Thank you, Joe.)

2. The smaller the steps, the easier the journey.

3. Keep your list in something obvious, like a spiral notebook. Why make a list on a scrap piece of paper that will get lost in the midst of clutter, hurry, or confusion? (Or in little hands that might scurry your list away.)

4. If a specific chore on a daily list isn't completed, bump it onto the next day's list. You will be astonished by your accomplishments once you learn this principle.

5. Be flexible enough to erase something if need be.

6. Be realistic—you may not be in a situation that lends itself to much organization right now. Tiny steps will do just fine.

7. Use the list. As you begin to cross off your daily accomplishments, you will begin to experience a sense of stewardship and be utterly amazed by how much extra time you've discovered.

Find Time to Take Life Seriously

Have you ever taken time to seriously evaluate your life? If not, you *need* a meeting; if yes, this new concept may be right up your alley.

This idea may not seem feasible if you live alone, yet I encourage you to have a "meeting of one" regardless of how foolish it may sound. If you live with other adults or a married partner, I cannot stress enough the value of having a regular meeting to discuss plans and dreams.

Joseph and I try to meet monthly. We actually purchased special notebooks and pens that are kept only for the purpose of our meetings. And we never meet at home. We always find a spot away from our own digs to hold our meetings. We even meet when traveling. (We once had a New Year's Day meeting at a French café in Alexandria, Virginia, that lasted *four hours*...and necessitated the consumption of several gooey pastries.)

So what do two people who live together and talk to each other *all the time* discuss at their meetings? Dreams, mostly. Having a specific time to dream somehow makes what we have to say more vital and more plausible. We think through to logical extensions of our plans, relationships, career choices, and financial situation. We factor in everything during our structured meeting because none of life exists in a vacuum. Each decision affects several other decisions. A clear vision motivates us to make our dreams come true.

A typical meeting might be held at a local coffee shop. Out come the notebooks and pens. Our meeting starts with prayer and is divided into several categories: health and hygiene, pets, careers, future, budget, travel, home care, friends and family, our spiritual walk, our love life, personal improvement, and hobbies.

We inscribe the date and location, and then we begin with our first category. We both write our ideas, feelings, successes, and failures. Next, we share what we wrote, and then we come to agreement on how we will approach that issue during the next month. This automatically turns monthly meetings into *review*. We share many burdens or concerns during these important meetings, which have become effective tools to manage not just money but every aspect of our lives, always to the glory of God. About the only rules we follow are to listen as the other speaks and to try to stay cool regardless of what is said. This is not always easy. (*All* things, whether organizing a shoe rack or keeping one's cool, get better with practice and resolve.) Our marriage has benefited much from these meetings.

Be sure to be rested, healthy, and as stress-free as possible when you meet. If we try to meet when we are tired, sick, or cranky, we are asking for disaster.

Finding Time: Twosies & Threesies

Twosies and threesies is a silly little method of mine for getting things done—and saving a remarkable amount of time. Here is how it works:

When I am busy doing any number of chores (let's say daily household chores), I operate with two or three things in my mind at once. And just as I have lists to help me plan my trips when doing chores outside the home, so I strategically plan my inside chores. I tend to those tasks that are time sensitive first: If dinner needs to defrost, out comes dinner; if laundry needs to be done, in goes a load so it washes while I tend to other chores.

Thinking things through is important as I "cluster" chores to be done.

Let's say I have to feed the dog, put clothes in the dryer, and haul something upstairs. My mind will think like this: *dog, dryer, upstairs*. Let's say the thing I'm hauling upstairs goes in our bedroom, and the bed isn't made. As soon as the dog is fed, my mind jumps to *dryer, upstairs, bed*. It may be that the trash in my bathroom as well as the dishwasher in the kitchen need emptying. Which room is closest to the bedroom? The bathroom is next to the bedroom, so my mind thinks *upstairs, bed, bathroom trash*. Then my automatic pilot shifts to *bed, trash, dishwasher*.

This is not as tricky as it sounds! It keeps me focused on what needs doing and gets it done in a surprisingly efficient manner. Do I run around with twosies and threesies in my head all the time? *Sheesh!* I'm not a fanatic, remember?

Just Do It

Having something on a list is smart. Letting it go undone is not smart. So let's go back to attitude again. Who is to say *why* we don't do things that we should? Remember what the apostle Paul said? "For what I want to do I do not do, but what I hate I do" (Romans 7:15). Hang this message onto everything else in this chapter: *just do it.*

I have found over and over that something gets done when I simply *do* the thing. The sentiment may sound silly, but in the time I've typed this section I could have made my bed, cleaned the top tray in the dishwasher, or straightened my desk. Sometimes we don't tackle a task because we are immobilized by the *number* of things that must be done—yet if we just *did* the task, we'd be astonished by how little time it took.

Someone I know once said, "There is no such thing as not enough time." I think he was right. We have no problem finding or making time for things we like to do (or to see, as in the case of a favorite TV show). Finding time is a simple matter of prioritization. Unless, of course, you are a mother of small children, in which case you should ignore all of this and go eat a quart of raspberry ripple ice cream.

> *Smart Think:*
>
> How much time do I spend watching television or playing mind-numbing games on the computer?

Time-Saving Techniques

■ Make the bed in 30 seconds or less. A made bed does wonders for the psyche; walking into a bedroom when the bed is neat feels good. For some reason, making the bed sets us on better footing for the day. It should not be a production to make your bed. If you are a crazed pillow collector, pare down. Sure, designers crowd a bed with pillows of every conceivable size and design, especially when the bedroom is in a photo shoot. Well, those designers don't have to sleep in that bed! Or to make it every day in the midst of noisy children, a lost sock (it's in the pile on the closet floor), and ringing telephones. Moving the pillows so you can crash at night is a nuisance. Where do they usually go, anyway? On the floor, where they pick up dog hair and dust bunnies. I recommend that your bed have two sleeping pillows, two top pillows covered with decorative shams, and maybe one extra designer pillow for contrast and texture. You might consider using a duvet (easily made using two sheets) as a case for your comforter or blanket.

Invest 30 seconds in your day: Straighten the sheets, fluff the pillows, fold the duvet down halfway to give the bed an inviting look. *Shazam.* Bed made.

- Doing the laundry. Putting away clean laundry is my least favorite thing to do. When I really want to be efficient and save time, I bring clean laundry to the room where it will be hung or stored. As I fold clothes, they immediately go into dresser drawers or closets.

- Put things away right away. The reason you don't hang your coat in the closet is because the closet is too jammed. Make room. Then hang your coat when you come in.

- Invest in a feather duster or one of those new-fangled fuzzy static-electric dusters. Slip some music in the CD player, and in the time it takes Celine Dion to sing "My Heart Will Go On," you can give your house the once-over—enough to hold it until serious cleaning.

- Make one trip. Whether I am emptying the dishwasher, hauling items downstairs, or heading to the car, I try to make one trip—and I never, *ever* go empty-handed. We have two market baskets upstairs. Anything relegated to the basement goes in or near the baskets. When I am headed downstairs, a basket goes with me. Sigh…getting Joseph to master this "one trip" notion is another story…

The Adventures of Wonder Man

Try as I may, I cannot convince Wonder Man to bring his lunch bucket inside when he comes home from work…empty-handed. He evidently prefers fetching it when temperatures plummet and he needs a snow shovel, mukluks, and flashlight to get to his truck. Maybe I can coax him to read this chapter.

～ ～ ～

Time-Saving Tips

- Don't depend on memory! Write things down.

- Every time you look up a number in the phone book, underline the number.

- Try to get the doctor's first appointment of the day.

- Call in your prescription so you don't have to wait at the pharmacy.

- Ask a store if it will preassemble something you've purchased without charging a fee.

- Provide each family member a separate shelf or basket for toiletries to avoid wasting time digging for your own things.

- Learn to say no and learn to set realistic deadlines.

- Designate a "household key center," and do not set your keys anywhere else. Have backup keys strategically hidden.

- Establish a weekly family planner. Analyze a sample week and determine when and why you melt down, as well as how you can make your week more manageable.

- Get enough sleep.

- Clean up as you work. This cuts down on a huge amount of effort spent scrubbing stains and sorting through piles.

- Always confirm appointments.

- If you live in an area where rush-hour traffic is an issue, try to commute to work a tad earlier. Better yet, see if you can begin and end your workday a little earlier.

- Try to do as much as possible by phone.

- Set aside time to prepare groceries as you store them after shopping. For instance, cut some meat into serving sizes before freezing it, trim some radishes and put them into a container with a folded paper towel, and wash and dry your apples before putting them in the veggie bin.

CHAPTER 5

It Pays to Be Savvy

The Adventures of Frugal Woman

Because "Never buy retail!" has become my mantra, I'm attracted to a bargain like bathrobe lint to a black skirt. I can't help it; it's genetic. Some of us who salivate at the mere suggestion of a sale must cope with this condition, which medical science has named *Discountis Amongus*.

When an attack hits, adrenaline pumps bold corpuscles through our pocketbook and sets our jaw in firm resolve. It's a fatal attraction kind of thing. Take a recent weekend, for example.

What we intended to be a leisurely trip away from home, a lovely ride through yonder countryside, an unhurried holiday as we explored heretofore uncharted parts of a neighboring state, became a moment that we will remember in the sweet warmth of victory: I stumbled upon the most unbelievable closeout sale on the planet. Fortunately, Wonder Man was along to protect me. This was one of those rare times when shopping turns to duty and challenge. I was up to the task.

Discountis Amongus is mostly gender exclusive. Women of every size and variety approached this closeout sale with The Look. The right brain is locked into arithmetic mode, prepared to calculate percentage-off prices with IBM precision. The eyes are focused on color and size (Hubby: "I'm going out to sit by the lake." Wife: "Lake?"). The hands are free of unnecessary clutter to enable easy access to racks and shelves (with fingernails sharpened for peak performance during the inevitable "I saw it first!" episode). Slip-on shoes, tights, and a tee-shirt allow shoppers to wiggle into otherwise-unacceptable sizes. All ears are on red alert.

I was in this mode when I heard a clerk whisper to her companion that *three more boxes* of clearance items were on their way from the warehouse. The woman next to me (clearly an apprentice, what with her meek demeanor) eyed my every move, sensing, I am sure, that she was in the presence of greatness. I acted nonchalant and detached as I worked my way to the counter. "Ho-hum," I yawned, keeping my eye on the door. The boxes were wheeled in. My muscles were as tense as a crouching tiger's. *Steady*...I pretended to occupy myself with...well, I *think* it was an ink smudge on the counter. The boxes were unloaded. Tension filled the air. My timing had to be impeccable. The woman pushing the dolly turned to leave. It had to be...*now!* I sprang. Sprang and ripped, actually, pulling fat strapping tape with my fingernails, with my hands, with my teeth... "Joseph! Bring me your pocketknife!" That was a lethal mistake. While my husband tried to fight his way into the store, a woman who brought new meaning to 3XL flattened me. She blocked for the others. Not willing to give ground, I dove headfirst into the nearest box. Regrettably, one woman mistook me for an upside-down mannequin and tried to pry off my shoes.

"What if it's ripped?" called one woman. The hapless clerks announced they would practically *pay* us to take it. This whipped us all into delirium.

"Joseph!" I yelled to my husband who was still far back and stationed at the door. "Catch this!" A dress flew through the air, intercepted by Ms. Meek, who was blind-sided by Big Bertha. Joseph cut right for a pass. A rust-colored sweater rocketed his way. Face mask from Meek and Mild—bummer of a day not to have a helmet. He broke wide. A pair of shoes sailed through the air. Touchdown!

"But they are two different styles!" Joe yelled. Not to worry, I assured him, they were both brown—with a pair of slacks, no one would notice. I pointed as a clerk heaped a new batch on a shelf. Ms. Meek-Turned-Crazed elbowed me out of the way and bulldozed a tie rack as she barreled by. This was war.

"But you don't wear size 5!" said hubby, carefully. "Not to worry," I assured him. We were both going on a diet on Monday morning.

One woman was quite civil, actually. I could tell she was a veteran of such events by her advanced technique. Our teamwork was something to behold as we neared each other from separate ends of the same rack. One of the great moments in shopping history—we engaged in a flawless execution of the under-over maneuver. I passed under her armpit as we each continued our rack search without as much as a break in rhythm.

Ah. It was a windfall weekend. A once-in-a-lifetime happenstance. Serendipity. The stuff of dreams. Now if only I could lose some weight.

Cents and Savvy

A little hyperbole—but a fairly accurate story! That weekend episode happened six years ago and still brings a smile. It can be fun, you know, to go a little crazy at those once-in-a-lifetime moments. Poking fun at our crazed behavior is just as enjoyable. For the record, I never did lose enough weight, but I had an awesome outfit to present my sister for her birthday. The clearance sale, after all, was at a high-end clothing store, and I would have been foolish to pass a chance to stock my gift closet with quality merchandise. In other words, I saw a real bargain, I had room to spare in our clothing and gift budgets, and I pounced. Note that we didn't set out on the weekend with shopping in mind.

The purpose of this chapter is to demonstrate the importance of becoming a savvy consumer and knowing prices so that when you stumble upon a sale, you will know whether you should pounce or merely sniff it out and walk away.

These skills, developed over time, will shave hundreds of dollars from your yearly outgo. As a bonus, you will have fun, you will shop to shop (not for recreation or because of boredom), you will satisfy most of your needs, and you will relish the thrill of victory.

With Tightwads on one side of the street and folks with Born to Shop emblazoned on their ball caps on the other, this chapter will blast right down the middle of the highway. By following my seven easy principles, you will prove you don't have to make your own soap or spin your own wool to survive on one income. You will show you can have a credit card as long as you are responsible and can elevate "savvy consumer" to an art form.

These are my seven principles:

1. Learn prices.

2. Shop to shop, not to drop.

3. Buy wisely.

4. Watch all register tallies and receipts.

5. Politely return when necessary.

6. Give salespeople ownership.

7. Shop in season.

Smart Think:

An item is not a bargain if you don't really need it or can't fit into it.

There is no risk whatsoever in telling you that if you employ these principles, you are guaranteed to make one paycheck go further than it has before.

Learn Prices

Few rules are more important than this one if you want to save money. Whether you're shopping for a jar of pickles or a VCR, a long-distance phone call or a car, learn prices! *Know a good buy.* With this rule, practice makes perfect. Start small and learn the regular price and the sale price of items you purchase often.

Joseph and I will commonly wait months or *years* before we purchase something on our "Get" list. Our computers are perfect examples. Since anything that buzzes, beeps or blinks, and plugs in is my husband's domain (I have held a two-by-four to my computer and made vicious threats), Joe took his time before we invested in either of our computers. (Joe inherited my original computer when I needed an upgrade.)

Joe visited with computer jocks, stopped at stores, read information, talked to a whole lot of people, and got bids. He is like that. Whether he is looking for a used car, a cell phone, or a laptop, Joe knows a good price when one comes his way. What may at times appear to be impulse is actually recognition of an elusive deal.

Learning Prices

Time and experience have already taught you a few things about items you buy on a regular basis. You can also take some practical measures to speed your education.

A good place to start is with your grocery bill. By studying the weekly fliers that come with your newspaper, you will develop confidence with pricing and recognize a steal of a deal instantly. Your newspaper is actually a wonderful tool.

For instance, if you are beginning to think about a different vehicle, spend a few weeks reading the Automobiles listing in the Classified section and studying dealer ads. In addition, you might call your local bank or go to the library to consult the *Blue Book,* which gives the suggested values of cars. The Internet can be invaluable when learning prices, as well.

A test run through various car dealerships will further inform you about prices. Keep your guard up, however—I'm convinced there is something added to the new-car smell that gets us every time (the evil side of aromatherapy)!

Learning Credit Card Prices

Any talk about being savvy and learning prices would be incomplete without mention of credit cards. When used responsibly, credit cards can be an advantage. Just be careful. The credit business is highly profitable for the issuing card company *as long as you stay in debt.* The combination of interest, cash advance charges, and other fees gives the credit-card issuers billions of dollars of profit each year. Billions of your dollars.

Seductive offers come by mail and offer to ease your credit crunch by promising lower introductory interest rates. But the fine print contains clauses that would curl your toes.

Do some research to determine the best credit card to have. Consumer magazines often dedicate an issue to the status of credit, and credit cards, in our country.

Smart Think:

Fine print often takes away what large print offers.

Check with the bank or credit union you do business with. Tell them you are shopping. You should follow two rules about credit cards:

1. *No annual fee.* The only credit card you should be willing to pay an annual fee for these days is a co-branded card. You should not have to pay an annual fee on any other card. The competition for your dollar is too great. If you are paying a fee, call your company and announce you would like the card for free. Under a co-branded system, credit card firms team up with car makers, airlines, and other businesses to offer rebates or incentives (frequent flier miles, money off the next car) to card members. Co-branded cards usually charge an annual fee.

2. *A low interest rate.* If you have a high rate now, call your company and tell them you want a lower rate. If they say no, ask to speak to a manager. If you still get a no, wait a day and call again (you will get another person). If you can't get a lower rate, find another card company. Of course, if you are a responsible card user, interest rates will be unimportant because you are paying your bill in full each month.

Beware! Most store credit cards are not recommended for two reasons. First, they usually charge the highest interest rates. Second, they don't offer broad usage.

Gimmicks a Savvy Consumer Will Avoid

Mary Hunt has written excellent books to help people with money management. In an article for *Focus on the Family Magazine*, she warned of credit card company ploys:

■ *Skip a payment* means more interest for the company.

■ *A check in the mail* is nothing but a high-interest loan, many with interest that accrues daily!

■ *Deferred billing* is based on statistics that say you will buy more if you don't have to pay now. Besides, chances are slim to zero that you will be in a better position to pay next year.

Shop to Shop, Not to Drop

Going shopping is okay. If we all stopped shopping, we would not be able to meet our needs, local merchants who depend on our trade would go bankrupt, and our national economy would suffer. No one wants to be responsible for that!

I am proposing that you don't shop unless necessary. As I've asked before, what usually happens when you go into a store? You buy something! *So don't go into a store.* At least not without reason.

I once was methodical in my food shopping. A long time ago, yes, and my practice was to shop on Wednesdays, the day weekly sales began. I'd study newspaper ads with the dedication of a Rhodes scholar, and I knew my stuff! I bought things *because they were on sale,* toted them home, and put them on a shelf. Until I got wise.

Mom and I liked to make an afternoon of visiting thrift stores in our area. It was a fun outing for us. Guess what? I rarely left any thrift store without something tucked under my arm. I got wise there, too.

Unless you are Ebenezer Scrooge (in which case you wouldn't be in a store to begin with), you will *always* find something to tote home when you go shopping. So, don't. Unless you have to.

Smart Think:

Calm down, cool off.
You can *always* find a sale.

Buy Wisely

Let's look at want versus need, at quality, and at quantity.

Do you buy things you want or things you need? This simple question is not so easy to answer.

Proponents of need-only buying are either living a truly threadbare existence in which even needs may go unmet, or they are stoic in their philosophy and choose to live sacrificially. If their sacrifice is not at the expense of others (such as family members), and if their sacrifice is to the overall benefit of others (philanthropy), then such an undemanding and simple lifestyle is commendable. I live in constant struggle with satisfying my basic needs for shelter, food, and safety while many would consider such basic comforts a luxury. Living our cushy lives and overlooking the despair of others is far too easy. I believe smart use of our finances is a responsibility we bear not just to ourselves, but toward the disenfranchised in our world. We must never forget that. Beside limitations of one income, it is this very responsibility that motivates many of us to want to live and spend wisely. So let's get back to needs and wants.

> The rich and poor meet together: the LORD is the maker of them all.
>
> —PROVERBS 22:2 KJV

I remember a moment at least 20 years ago when Joseph, our son, Joshua, and I were walking along a street in the high-rent district of Seattle, Washington. "Look at that expensive house," I said sarcastically, "and the expensive car in the driveway! Think how much of that money could go to the needy rather than on such luxury!" I was high and mighty. Joshua spoke: "Mom, how do you know that person doesn't tithe 90 percent of his or her income?"

Good question, Son. The point is this: For whatever reason, our sovereign God has allowed some in this world to have wealth, sufficient funds, or comforts not enjoyed by others. The love of money, *not its wise use,* is sin. So what about want? Can you simply *want* something, no "needy strings" attached? We fulfill our wants all the time. It is excess, greed, stupidity, and covetousness that we must avoid. Can a want that has nothing to do with essentials be considered a need? A need for the beauty of art, a need for the soothing harmony of great music, a need for a serene, comfortable, and attractive home? I believe it can as long as it is wise and does not become obsession, or sin.

Think about this:

- You don't *need* an ice-cream cone—after all, you could stay home and eat gruel—but it brings pleasure.

- You don't *need* a Sunday afternoon ride through the country—after all, you could stay home and stare at your walls—but it connects your soul to creation.

- You don't *need* to rent a family-friendly video and make popcorn—after all, you could sit in your stark living room and twiddle your thumbs—but it is a definite bonding experience. Besides, you actually *did* need the downtime and laughter.

> It is not a sin to have riches, but it is a sin to fix our hearts on them.
>
> —JOHN BAPTISTE DE LA SALLE

Quality

Places such as dollar stores and major discounters can be very smart places to shop *if* you consider quality. Buying something so inferior in quality that it will not serve its function properly, or will break in record time, makes no sense. That would be, as the saying goes, "penny wise and pound foolish." I occasionally shop at such stores, but I have developed an eye for that which will last.

If you know prices and find a good deal, be sure to check quality. What does the label say? How will the garment lay on the body? What do the hinges look like? Is particleboard used? How will this product hold up? If it's an inexpensive tool, is it of inferior strength? What do the ingredients say about what I'm serving my family? Is there a warranty of any merit? Am I familiar with the brand? Can it be cleaned? Is it dangerous?

How can something, inferior or not, be dangerous? Think of children's toys, infant furniture, cheap candles. (Cheap candles are not only a royal mess but they can also burn erratically and pose a fire threat.)

You needn't buy top of the line, and sometimes we can't. But try hard to put your money to work for you and to buy intelligently. Thrift stores can be treasure troves when looking for quality labels in clothing.

On a recent trip to Virginia we found a magnificent bureau in mint condition—handcrafted with fine wood. It had been shoved into the back room of a used-furniture store, and sold for *less* than one of those particleboard models at the big discount store. (By asking the simple questions you will soon learn, we purchased the bureau for $50 less than its already low price.)

Smart Think:

There is a 50/50 chance you will buy something if you pick it up to examine it. That is one reason some markets put the price on an item rather than on a shelf.

Quantity

The price per ounce or per pound of food is often posted on the lip of market shelves. Learn to read them. Don't, for heaven's sake, invest in a greater quantity unless it is something you will use in the next year or so. Warehouse stores can get you on this one! Paying an extra 50 cents for one can of sardines in a supermarket makes more sense than paying an extra five dollars to purchase ten cans that you will never, *ever* use but for one recipe.

On the flip side, you can buy an entire block of cheese for what you pay for a lesser amount that is pre-sliced or shredded.

Here's one more suggestion about quantity. We Americans seem to be smitten with extra-large and grande. Remember that latte we talked about at the beginning of the book? Not only should you try skipping a day at the coffee shop, but also, next time you go, order the small cup. Ditto next time you order fries. Or a pizza, if there are not too many of you. Learn to sip and nibble. We don't chew our food long enough, anyway.

Watch Register and Check Receipts

Never, *ever* stand idly by without watching as your prices are rung up on the cash register! If you are overwhelmed with children or a big load of groceries, pick a checkout line that will cause less stress, use a familiar clerk, or ask that prices be entered or scanned only when you can watch.

I know clerks get testy. I know you might feel anxious or embarrassed, but you *can* do this. If you can't monitor the cash register, check your receipt in the car or at home. This is an important principle. I've caught busy clerks accidentally scanning the same item twice *many* times. We were once charged $70 for shampoo. It was an easy mistake to catch, but I shudder to think how much money we might donate to stores because of human and scanner error at the checkout. This is especially true when you are in a store that announces a percentage off already marked prices. These stores usually have a mob of people and long lines because of a spectacular sale. Take the time to figure a general total either on note paper or in your head, and watch like a hawk. Mistakes happen. If you find a mistake, speak up—politely, of course.

The Adventures of Frugal Woman

Was it a swindle? There I was, laden with luggage, a long line behind me. The clerk handed me my coffee and said $2. I politely pointed to the sign that said $1.25.

Down the airport concourse I went, and I purchased a souvenir for $2.95. The clerk asked for $4.59. Even with tax, I knew that was wrong.

Want to venture a guess how many times both you *and* I have just complied and handed over our moolah?

～ ～ ～

Politely Return (and Politely Complain)

Be polite!

If you have purchased a product that has failed to meet its proper function, has gone bad, or has not held up within reason, take it back. (Inexpensive electronics are legendary in this regard.) This is not a principle to abuse, nor is it a principle that should promote dishonesty on the part of a consumer. But puh-*leeze*, return something rather than let the store keep your money while you keep something you will not or cannot use.

This principle applies to service as well. Pray for the wisdom of Solomon, and kindness and patience as well. But if you have paid perfectly good money for a perfectly rotten meal or motel room or plane ride, have a little chat with the chef, manager, or public relations department. I send letters. In my letters I document as much as I can: the date, the time of day, the server or clerk, and the reason for my dissatisfaction. Sometimes I receive a certificate for future dining, lodging, or travel. At other times I receive an apology with no refund. Occasionally I receive nothing for my efforts.

A recent example comes from an otherwise fine dinner with our son, in the Washington, D.C., area. The service was impeccable, the surroundings were clean. But I got sick, and it was unmistakably food poisoning. My holiday in Washington was shortened by two days in bed. A polite letter ensued. And so did a full refund for our meal. This was a matter of my word against theirs, and it resulted in quite an extraordinary gesture from that establishment. My point is, why on earth would I pay anyone hard-earned money to make me ill?

Don't be fearful of returning an item for the right reason or for communicating politely about the quality and service you have paid for.

Ownership

Joseph teases that he is going to have an alarm made to warn store clerks and managers that I am in the vicinity. He says this following me around as I sniff out deals. I have long used a system which I call "ownership," and I am excited to share this with you. It is probably my number one favorite principle toward becoming a savvy consumer: *I ask*. Ask what, you say?

When I enter a store, I make a beeline for the back, where clearance racks are situated. I scan the signs and determine whether the store is even worth my time. Just how good are their sales, anyway? If I decide to stick around, I give a clerk (preferably a floor manager) *ownership* by asking one of these questions:

- "Hi, there," I say with a truly sincere smile. "What is the most amazing sale in your store today?"

- "Hi, there. What one thing is on sale in this store for such an amazing price that even you can hardly believe it?"

- "Hi, there. I'm looking for something in your fishing lure department (for example), and I am really limited on how much I can spend. It's a gift for my son."

- "Hi, there. Is there anything in your store that is marked down due to damage or blemish?"

- "Hi, there. Are you the manager? I don't mean to put you on the spot, and I feel a tad sheepish about asking, but would you look at a certain item I've found on your floor and tell me if I am entitled to a reduction in price due to blemish?"

- "Hi, there. Are you the manager? I feel a tad sheepish about this question, but can you do better on this price?"

You have to try this to believe the success you will have. Above all, remember this: You are not entitled to what you are asking. You are merely asking. Clerks and store managers and store owners have often told me about the rude and demanding nature of customers. You dare not be rude. And please understand that "no" is as much an answer to your question as "yes."

Shop Seasonally

If you want to slash your food budget, learn the law of supply and demand. Shop for groceries when they are in season. Because the supply of a product might outweigh the demand, prices drop when markets have an abundance of certain foods. For instance, when there is a glut of oranges because of a bumper crop, the price of oranges falls. The opposite is also true: When the crop hasn't yet been harvested, or when it has been damaged or destroyed, the price goes up.

"Seasonal" does not always refer to harvest. Holidays and life cycles also have an effect on prices. For instance, when children go back to school, you may see a jump in the price of bananas because bananas are a lunch box staple. Bananas, however, will usually go down in price during holidays, when people need them for baking. President's Day, Veteran's Day, Thanksgiving, Christmas, St. Patrick's Day, Easter, and the Fourth of July all bring special prices.

I plan several south-of-the-border meals in spring to celebrate the fifth of May (Cinco de Mayo). In summer, I present platters of sliced radish, cucumber, and tomato with a chunk of bread. I serve apple cobbler in autumn. (Word of warning! In early fall, ask your grocer if the fabulous sale on apples or potatoes is *this year's crop*. Way too often the answer will be "no." Why? Producers clear out warehoused produce to make room for new crops. It's true.)

As with bananas, sometimes demand brings prices up rather than down. Meat is a perfect example. Though stores occasionally offer sensational sales, certain cuts of meat go *up* in price when they are most in demand. Heavier cuts of meat such as roasts are more expensive in winter when they are simmered all day as comfort food. Grill meats such as steaks go *up* when the charcoal comes out of the garage. As bonuses to buying food seasonally, you will expand your cooking abilities by creating meals around seasonal foods, you will expand your eating pleasure by experimenting with different recipes, and you might benefit nutritionally from the quality of the foods you eat.

Just because asparagus (for instance) plummets in price from late March to June doesn't mean you must go without the rest of the year: Learn to freeze, dehydrate, or can produce that is in season.

Seasonal Sales

January

Food: standing ribs, steaks, chicken, pork, grapefruit, party foods

Other: amazing sales due to holiday excess

February

Food: steaks, citrus, young turkeys

Other: furniture, home furnishings, lease-return cars, audio-visual equipment, men's apparel, air conditioners

Watch for Valentine's Day and President's Day sales.

March

Food: corned beef, cabbage, fresh fish

Pay attention: Many markets increase cost on some produce because supplies diminish.

Other: garden supplies, winter sports equipment, laundry detergent, infant wear

April

Food: Mexican foods (last week of month), ham, eggs

Other: white sales (linens and tablecloths), TV or VCR, hosiery, painting supplies, stoves, lingerie, cleaning products, off-season rates at some resorts

May

Food: Mexican food (first week), roasts, asparagus, strawberries, Texas onions

Other: baskets, clocks, knives, silverware, musical equipment, power tools, small appliances, luggage

June

Food: beginning of hot-dog wars, early melons, corn, picnic foods, ketchup

Other: charcoal, paper plates

July

Food: Fourth of July specials, hamburger, corn, bell peppers

Other: beachwear, fabric, fuel, men's shoes and shirts

August

Food: produce, marshmallows (think popcorn balls at Christmas)

Other: sports equipment, garden furniture, nursery plants (trees and perennials)

September

Food: apples, winter squash, end of barbecue and picnic season

Other: paint, school supplies, office supplies

Buy Christmas and birthday presents at summer closeouts. Watch for car clearances. The best time to buy a car is at the end of a month.

October

Food: candy sales end of month, baking supplies, apples, hard-skinned squash

Other: white sales, tire wars, camping gear

November

Food: baking supplies, cranberries (can be frozen right in the bag for future muffins)

Watch for loss-leader blow-outs around Thanksgiving.

Other: *Watch for Veteran's Day sales. The day after Thanksgiving is notorious as the busiest shopping day of the year—watch for early-bird sales.*

December

Food: baking supplies, nuts, bananas, boneless chuck, potatoes, yams

Other: coats, children's wear, power tools, blankets and quilts

Watch for phenomenal sales between Christmas and New Year's, as well as throughout the month. Early in the month, thrift stores display ornaments, toys, sleds, winter wear, skis and skates. The good selection goes fast.

Retail Dateline

A friend who runs several hundred miles each year goes through several pairs of running shoes. When he finds his shoes for less than half off, he purchases two pairs and puts one in his closet...*that* is a savvy consumer. He knows when to find shoes on sale because he knows the retail dateline.

Are you amused when you see bathing suits on sale before the snow melts, school clothes on display while you are basking by the pool, and ski boots advertised when you are raking leaves? Welcome to the retail dateline! Retailers celebrate the Fourth of July at Easter, winter in summer, and Halloween on Labor Day. If a store has to be 100 percent "back to school" by July, the racks of bathing suits, beach towels, and shorts have got to go. But the stores have no place to send them! Aha! You will end up with summer clothes drastically reduced starting around the beginning of July. Get it?

Want a general guideline to the dateline? Start watching for spring clothing closeouts around the last week in April. Watch for any holdover spring, as well as all summer clothing, to close out around the last week in July. Most fall and all back-to-school clothes should close out around the end of October, and winter clothes and the holiday season get slashed around the end of January. (Incidentally, just about everything in a store will sport a 25-percent-off ticket at some time during its shelf life.)

"Clean up in season" is a sacred phrase in retail. It means items with a seasonal application must be sold during that season or holiday time. Consider Valentine's Day, the most costly day for retail stores. Buying inventory for this holiday is difficult. Why? What's a merchant to do with two dozen heart-shaped boxes of candy on February 15?

I am not a big fan of Halloween, but just the other day I walked into an upscale coffee shop and saw lovely ceramic pumpkins positively *slashed* in price. The date was November 1.

A good department store will be out of seasonal merchandise at the peak of the season. If you wait until out-of-stock price slashing, the nice selection will be long gone. However, retailers dramatically reduce prices on goods that have lingered beyond the peak selling period.

If you are patient, trips with your list to the mall (several department stores) during any of the projected out-of-stock sales will probably net you a terrific buy. These are great—no, make that *fabulous*—opportunities to buy Christmas or birthday gifts at significant savings.

Know your correct size, color, and style. At one time, I would buy something if a) it fit, b) it was a great deal, and c) it was good quality. Sometimes I looked good in what I bought; sometimes I perpetuated my image as Queen of the Dorks. Over time I learned to avoid certain colors. Not too long ago, I learned to avoid fit and style that were unbecoming to my body type. Until then I'd reasoned incorrectly that if I wore a big, baggy dress, I would hide any bulges. Wrong. Only made me look larger.

I invested in a book called *Flatter Your Figure* by Jan Larkey (Simon & Schuster, 1992). Now I pay attention to styles that will flatter my figure. It took me a while to get smart about this, but little by little I am creating a classic, timeless wardrobe that fits me just right!

Savvy Shopping Strategies

General Info

- Everything in a convenience store is expensive. Almost everything in a convenience store is bad for your health.

- Do not do business over the phone unless you initiate the transaction.

- "Buy one, get one free" can be a gimmick. A 32-ounce brand-name jelly was recently advertised with the offer, "Buy one, get one free; save $1.85 on two." That same jar of jelly commonly sells for less than a dollar. And generic brands can often beat that price.

- Don't get same-day or one-hour service for anything unless you absolutely have to.

■ If you can't afford to pay the full cost of something you need, consider buying it used.

■ Avoid unnecessary catalog buying. Catalog buying is usually more expensive, and you can't try anything on. I once bought a long black corduroy shirtdress from a catalog. When I put it on, I looked like a Greek olive with feet.

Travel

■ Airport and municipal fees can increase your car rental at an airport by 20 percent. You may be able to take the free shuttle to your hotel and rent a car from there at a lower price.

■ Want to tote home some exotic foods from a faraway place? Leave the tourist haunts and find a grocery store used by local folk.

■ Motels often cost more in metropolitan or resort areas. Thirty miles down the road, the same chain may be less expensive. Factor in transportation if the big city or resort is your destination.

Home Furnishings

■ A mattress is as good as its box spring. Up to 80 percent of your weight is borne by the box spring. You may be able to put a bit more money into the box spring and "spring" for a less expensive mattress.

■ The retail markup on furniture can be as high as 250 percent. Consider these options.

   1. Save up to 60 percent by buying returned overstock, scratch and dent, or older model merchandise.

2. Ask interior designers if they have inventory lingering in their back rooms.

3. Scout through a used-furniture store.

4. Look in your own attic.

■ Direct-from-the-mill carpet? Advertisements read: "Save up to 50 percent! Buy direct!" This can be money saving, but you must be wise and consider all of the expenses. Before you order, be sure to check...

1. cost of installation

2. cost of freight

3. cost of pads

4. cost of exact same carpet from local merchant

5. options if the carpet is flawed

Personal Items and Health

■ Healthy people, young or old, do not need vitamin drinks. Those drinks are a mixture of water, sugar, oil, milk and soy protein, plus a vitamin pill. Healthy people, young or old, need wholesome food. Eat a carrot and pocket the change.

■ Jewelry can be marked up as high as 300 percent.

■ Big bottles of shampoo may look like a bargain, but water is often the main ingredient.

■ Check to see if the community health department sponsors free medical tests, such as well-baby exams, mammograms, prostate checks, diabetes tests, and blood pressure tests.

■ Ask your doctor if generic drugs can be substituted on a prescription.

Sports and Hobbies

▨ Watch out! Music clubs, book clubs, and recipe card clubs add up to *big* bucks after you add shipping and handling. Suppose you join a recipe card club that ends up costing $8 each month. Suppose you bought those cards each month for one year. That's an expenditure of $96...more than enough for a splendid cookbook, without getting burned.

▨ Do your kids need expensive sports equipment? Do you need a bank loan just to keep the kids in sport shoes? Start a co-op. Use your garage as a sport-shoe consignment shop. Give donated shoes to less fortunate children.

Gifts

▨ When you see a sale item that would make a good birthday gift, buy a few so you don't have to shop each time your child is invited to a party.

▨ Buy inspirational books at reduced prices. They are perfect for last-minute gift giving.

▨ Did someone just come home from the hospital? Don't send flowers—make dinner.

▨ Is someone in the hospital? Don't send flowers—send a note that says you have cleaned her home, watered her plants, walked her dog.

(More gift ideas in chapter 9. Appendix 2 has a plethora of strategies and tips for food purchases.)

Store Savvy *Plus* Skill Savvy

Expenditures aplenty have nothing to do with walking into a store or learning the retail dateline. Our money goes to much

more than food and clothing. We also pay for services, professional or otherwise. The next chapter calls for some good old-
fashioned elbow grease as you learn to skirt the expense of
some of those services.

CHAPTER 6

Roll Up Your Sleeves

A Little Bit of Grit

*W*orking toward smart living on one income—and living well—is not for those who "low-impact" their way through life. It takes grit and determination and hard work. One reason we succumb to costly groceries is convenience and ease of preparation. It takes effort to cook from scratch! (Or so we all think.)

Our lives are busy and stress is high. We crave things that satisfy momentary needs to make life easier. We put off better discipline until tomorrow, but tomorrow never comes. If you are determined to develop smart money-saving habits, say hello to tomorrow today! Take a deep breath, roll up your sleeves, and expect to be a little busy.

> *Smart Think:*
>
> Today is the tomorrow I worried about yesterday.

Ever Watch an Ant?

Proverbs tells us to look to the ant: "Go to the ant, you sluggard; consider its ways and be wise! It has no commander, no overseer or ruler, yet it stores its provisions in summer and gathers its food at harvest" (Proverbs 6:6-8). It also gives us the creeps when it crawls into our potato salad, scurries on our kitchen counter, and runs up our sleeves...

Ever watch ants? The suckers never quit! And they *run* every place they go. I've seen ants race toward their hills, backs laden with pumpernickel bagels, German chocolate cake, whole watermelon, and corn dogs—Sherpa ants! Thank goodness we are told to *consider* the ant. We get the point, Lord. We don't have to scurry around with pumpernickel bagels on our backs, but we do have to gather, store, and be wise. The ant not only has no one peeking over its shoulder (if, indeed, ants *have* shoulders) but also doesn't hire out work that it can do itself. That is the message of this chapter: Be like the ant and *do it yourself.*

Do the mending, tending, cooking, cleaning, fixing, gardening, arranging, remodeling, and everything else that needs doing yourself. At least do as much as you can do by yourself without risking life, limb, or sanity.

The Adventures of Wonder Man

The dishwasher in our new home simply would not clean. Before I called the repairman, I called Wonder Man. He unscrewed three rotors from which the water sprays and cleaned the openings.

He found cherry pits, elbow macaroni, feathers (what did the previous owners wash in there?), pieces of glass, and tiny accumulations of minerals. The dishwasher has worked fine ever since.

Rubber Meets the Road

Rolling up your sleeves is right up there in the hit parade of principles that will save you money by the bundle: Learn to do things yourself, seek help so you can do things yourself, dig deep to find initiative to do things yourself, organize a plan to do things yourself, and *finish the things you began.* (Yes, I know you are chuckling right now.) Remember my appeal in the organization chapter for you to "just do it"? Now my appeal is to "just do it—squared!" Here's what I mean...

The view from our kitchen window was turning into an eyesore with one bird feeder of three looking pretty sorry. Paint was peeling, winter was coming, and the unprotected wood would suffer weather damage. I asked Joseph to paint the top of the feeder.

What would your reaction be if someone asked you to paint the roof of a bird feeder? Most of you would hem and haw, the project positively *huge* in your mind's eye. Paint? That's a big production! I mean, it takes days, weeks, *years!* Oh no, it doesn't. Ever make a sandwich?

To make a sandwich, you take ingredients from the fridge, right? You open a jar of mayonnaise, grab a knife, and spread. Then you put the lid back on your mayonnaise jar, wash the knife, and enjoy your sandwich. Ever paint the roof of a bird feeder?

You open the paint can, grab a paintbrush, and spread. Then you put the lid back on the paint can, wash the brush, and enjoy the view from the kitchen window. (You could even eliminate the cleaning step with a 35-cent foam paintbrush that you pitch away when finished.)

No one would hire a painting contractor to paint the top of a bird feeder. In most cases that feeder would have to wait a long, long time before it got attention, if it got painted at all. Too intimidating, painting. *Burp.* (Excuse me, I just finished my sandwich.)

This is as good a place as any to share one of the dumbest blunders of my do-it-yourself career: not marking paint cans. I have a collection of paint cans and no idea which

Smart Think:

Begin!
Half the work
is in the starting!

walls to match them with. What is the deal with us and half-used paint, anyway? Think about it. Nine times out of ten, when we repaint a room we paint it a different color.

Learn How to Do It Yourself

What's on your bookshelf? Novels, classics, sentimental favorites, poetry? Know what's on my bookshelf? One copy of just about every how-to book ever written. It's my thing. I would rather curl up with a book on do-it-yourself masonry than with a good thriller. Call it a chemical imbalance, but I've been this way from birth. When I was a kid, I didn't read dog or horse stories; I earnestly studied books about horse and dog *breeds,* how to shoe a horse, how to train a spaniel. All of this reading has turned me into a bit of an annoying know-it-all to close friends and family and has given me a whole lot of useless knowledge. Useless, that is, until a wire needs splicing, paneling needs hanging, a rock wall needs cementing, or a book crammed with ideas needs writing.

You don't have to donate your collection of Shakespeare to the local library to find room for a few such books. A handy fix-it manual, a cleaning manual, an interior design manual, a car care manual, a gardening manual, and several hundred thousand cookbooks should be all you need.

Whether you are faced with an emergency such as a gas leak, a basement flood, or a blown circuit, or you just want to tackle those hooks and shelves you've been meaning to install in the garage, you have only to turn to your bookshelf. You may quickly turn to the phone and call a pro once you've consulted your library, but at least you *considered* tackling a problem yourself. Remember the ant.

Men and women everywhere visit libraries to borrow how-to books and videos. They glue themselves to networks that offer home-improvement shows, join clubs or organizations to help them become better gardeners, and take evening courses at the local community college on everything from photography to auto mechanics.

We should not overlook the best teachers on the planet: Gram and Gramps. Remember them? Interrupt that snooze of theirs and ask them to share their skills, lore, and recipes with you. They will be thrilled and honored; you will be blessed.

See? You have plenty of ways to learn!

Seek Help

Now exactly how did Gramps tell me to join those two boards...?

Ohmygosh...did Gram tell me to use a dash of garam masala or a dash of dill?

Asking for help doesn't hurt. I've asked telephone repairmen to explain how I could splice some inside lines myself and written notes while they talked. I've sat through a few cooking classes, and one disastrous cake-decorating class where the instructor hit my knuckles with her wooden spoon when I licked my fingers. I've asked a friend to teach me a few crafty ideas. And as research for my first book, *1001 Bright Ideas to Stretch Your Dollars,* I've interviewed people at vacuum repair shops, tire shops, appliance repair shops, interior design shops, dry cleaners...you get the idea.

The first question I asked was, "What don't we know?"

The last question I asked was, "What is the single most important thing you want people to know about what you do?"

I still smile when I think about the response from the fellow at the tire shop: "Just because it's round and black doesn't mean it's the same."

To prove that I've sought help for my do-it-yourself compulsion, let me share a story from my teen years.

The Adventures of Frugal Teen

In 1967, I owned a 1956 grass green Volkswagen bug. I felt like a million bucks when I drove the Green

Hornet; it was the biggest and most valuable thing I'd ever owned, old and broken as it was. That thing could be fixed with piano wire! And it always needed fixing. It also needed body work. Rust had corroded one fender. I couldn't possibly pay a body shop for repair. What to do? For me it was as easy as a visit to a body shop and a six-pack of cola. I plopped down my bribe, blinked my baby gray green eyes, and asked if I could watch them work for a few hours. The pros not only let me watch, they told me exactly what fiberglass kit to buy and how to fix my fender.

As I recall, I did a horrid job; the fender was all bumpy with green paint that didn't quite match. So the Green Hornet sported a birthmark! At least the corrosion was stopped in its tracks. And I did it myself.

Times have changed. A visit to an auto body shop would now be restricted because of liability concerns, but my teenage adventure may give you the initiative to consult a pro for help with one of your projects.

~ ~ ~

Finding Initiative (Yawn)

This is a little like talking perfect world versus real world. Before I harp on initiative, let me issue a strong caveat. Please *consider* what I write here—and what I write in this entire book, for that matter! *Consider* whether investing the energy or effort for as little as a single project or as much as a change of philosophy is reasonable for you. I would never insist on "my way or the highway."

My fervent hope and prayer is that the suggestions in this book will help you to accomplish your financial goal of living comfortably on one income. Or even on two incomes. But you are not a superhero. Neither am I. I am merely on the path of least expenditure. I trip and take detours from time to time.

The last thing you need is a dose of guilt because you are not achieving "Maximum Thrift Potential" in the first 45 minutes! As a matter of fact, you should plan to relax all of these principles occasionally—otherwise, you set yourself up for failure, for a meltdown and a return to old systems, patterns, and habits. Remember, habits die hard.

Are you tired of your diet? Eat a candy bar and get back on the scale tomorrow. Tired of the constant push to be perfect in money management? Spend a little money (do try to spend it wisely) and go on a moratorium tomorrow.

Do not be surprised if you stumble or if you can't muster enough enthusiasm to clean that clog from your bathroom sink yourself. Tired of being savvy and organized and "doing it all by yourself?" Call a plumber.

On the other hand, initiative is just what you need if you are going to tackle projects on your own, and it has everything to do with attitude and time management. Once you rouse yourself and commit yourself to a project, it might not be as overwhelming as you once believed. Many household chores can be completed with time to spare, some in about the time it takes to make and eat a baloney sandwich.

Initiative sags because we are tired or lazy, for sure, but I believe the number one reason we lag in enthusiasm to accomplish our tasks is that we are overwhelmed by the big picture. We can hardly get excited about building a shelf if the rest of the garage looks like an obstacle course. The big picture can be daunting. Try to break it down to manageable parts with small victories.

For instance, clean one corner of the garage. Draw a line on the floor with chalk if you must, and vow to clean that one section so you have an ordered space for a few hooks. You will feel fabulous each time you pass that corner, and momentum may spring from this new beginning.

Plan How You Are Going to Do What You've Learned to Do

Before Joe painted the top of that bird feeder, he had a mental plan. He assembled the paint, paint can opener (*always* on a certain nail in his shop), a paint brush, and a short ladder. He most likely thought through the process of painting and did a dry run in his head. He may have wondered if the top needed cleaning from bird droppings. He may have considered the weather.

Whether you are painting a bird feeder, preparing a recipe, or building a dog house, think through your chore, assemble everything you will need from start to cleanup, factor in cost, and estimate a realistic amount of time to complete the project. (Is there a cook alive who hasn't prepared a new recipe for dinner that night only to get halfway through and read that it had to sit in the fridge overnight?)

Finish What You've Started

Finish? A collective groan can be heard from sea to shining sea, right? Women, let's talk about sewing projects, craft projects, and photo albums. For the men, I have two things to say: cleaning the garage and remodeling projects.

Smart Think:

Do I become paralyzed by the thought of how much time a task will take? Have I considered that most small chores can be accomplished either in a short amount of time or in bits of time, as long as I'm committed to completing the task?

Finishing work you've started is a huge success! I'm willing to bet that every person reading (or writing) this book has an unfinished project. (Mine? Photo album.)

It is easy to become distracted and hard to stay focused. Let's work on this issue together.

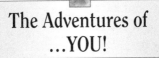

The Adventures of
...YOU!

When you awoke this morning, you had resolve. Two simple projects: prune the fruit trees and wash both cars. You never dreamed the weather would be dismal. The clouds are only a threat and the cold you can deal with, so the pruning comes first.

You drag a kitchen chair into the backyard and position it under the apple tree. A little uneven and tippy, but you're only a few feet off the ground. What could that hurt? How about your right knee when you take a belly flop on your first pass of the saw and slam your leg into a rock? Not to worry. You can patch the rip in your jeans (and thereby do things *yourself* like that woman who wrote that book said you should), and you aren't bleeding too badly.

Up you go again, but this time the blade from your neighbor's borrowed saw comes loose, and the screw lands someplace in the leaves beneath the tree. Not to be daunted, you ram the skinny tip of a chopstick into the hole and try to prune. No luck. So you hold the end of the saw with one hand, the other end in the other. No luck. You're beginning to get a little angry, so you try to rip the branch from the tree. Now you are hanging *over* your kitchen chair, which has itself done a belly flop into the leaves. You call for your child to move the kitchen chair so you don't completely mangle yourself when you drop three feet onto the ground, and the neighbor answers your call.

While the neighbor is wrapping his arms around your dangling legs, you engage in conversation about the college ball game, and you soon go inside to see who is winning. This leads to neighborly conversation during a short rainstorm in which the pruners, kitchen chair, and child get wet. The drop in humidity leads to a short snooze, after which you welcome Brother Sun and head out to wash the cars, not yet realizing that the nozzle to your hose was flattened by the garbage truck on Thursday morning.

~ ~ ~

Speaking of Children

Once you dry off your child, remember that it's never too early to teach a child *anything*. A foreign language, an ear for music, an appreciation of art, reasoning skills, work skills, and *smart money skills* are best learned at an early age. The child who grows on a solid foundation will enjoy an easier transition into adult responsibilities.

A child first learns by observation. Every single parent, grandparent, aunt, uncle, cousin, and friend knows firsthand that a child mimics what he or she has repetitively seen. This is distressingly clear when Junior lets rip an expletive-deleted at the church picnic.

Young children can be given easy tasks to perform. Kids' responsibilities should be child-friendly and manageable. For instance, a young child would be frustrated trying to neatly stack toys on a shelf; a big, open basket or box is more like it. The last thing you want to do is set a pattern of frustration for life!

By teaching age-appropriate versions of the principles in this book, you will help your children to become self-reliant, efficient, and productive members of their own future households—and of society.

Just be patient and willing to settle for child-quality work. If you are teaching a child to hammer, settle for a few bent nails. If you're cooking, settle for a lumpy batter; if you're painting, settle for some splatters on the floor...on the clothes...on the face...on the cat.

Ready to Roll Up Your Sleeves?

The logical question to ask yourself right now is, What do I pay others to do for me?

Next question: How much of that can I really do for myself, by myself, or with the help of others?

And finally, Is it worth my time, any stress the extra task might create, any hassles I may face due to the nature of the task?

There may be times when paying someone to do a chore for you is more sensible. (Something may need to be done when you just don't have any more sleeves to roll up!)

If you are out of town and your lawn must be mowed, pay to get the lawn mowed. If you are 13 months pregnant and can't bend over to wash the smelly poodle, pay the poodle groomer. If you are caring for an ill person and are about as strung out as a human being can get, pay for someone to clean your house. (The Ladies' Aid Society at your church would most likely happily provide helpful volunteers.)

What We Often Pay to Have Done

Here is a list of things we routinely pay for:

- laundry and ironing

- dry-cleaning

- house cleaning

- window washing

- snow removal

- lawn care and seasonal cleanup

- annual service to furnace

- chimney sweep

- pest control

- food to go

- car service including lube, oil, and filter; rotating tires; car wash

- haircut or hair color

- facial or body waxing

- manicures and pedicures

- massage

- pet grooming (I created a new breed once when I clipped the Spaniel. She wouldn't talk to us for weeks.)

- drain cleaning (inside pipes and outside gutters)

- knife sharpening

- shoe polishing

- carpet & upholstery shampoo

This list can be expanded almost infinitely when you consider bigger tasks, including plumbing, designing, painting, and remodeling.

The Adventures of Frugal Woman

I remember my first visit to one of those dollar stores...

I wandered around in a state of disbelief. How could something this wonderful be happening, here, just minutes from home? Consumer savvy began to kick in: Though only a dollar, much of what I saw was poor quality. But still! My heart stopped in the food aisle. There on the shelf was a favorite organic soup and the rye crackers Joseph and I prefer, both at significant savings. *This store could be a diamond in the rough,* I thought. I rounded a corner and saw *it.*

A burly man and I hit the display at the same time. His body language was unmistakable. The guy was clearly seasoned in advanced frugal matters. We both blinked and stood in amazement. There before our eyes was a stack of boxes, each containing a 26-pound bladder of tomato sauce. He looked at me, I looked at him, and we both looked at the sign on the wall: "Everything a dollar, folks!" I read and reread the printing on the boxes as a cold sweat began to form on my upper lip. He kicked a box for good measure. Trying to be cool, we both said "Hmmm."

Knees buckling, I looked as if I were toting a hundred-pound bowling ball as I struggled to my car. Home I went, bursting with satisfaction. Up went my sleeves, out came my canning equipment. Out also came onions, basil, garlic, and oregano. I canned several pints and quarts of "homemade" sauce. One of those pints sits on a shelf to this day, calico fabric and ribbon covering the lid, a trophy of sorts from my dollar-bargain jackpot.

Do-It-Yourself Groceries

Once you are aware of needless extra expense when purchasing food, you will find this rule an easy one to follow. You may be too busy to apply this principle at times, and that's okay. But don't automatically think you have to pay the grocer to do simple things for you!

Whenever you buy a product in the grocery store that has been prepared in any way, you are going to pay more money because someone has to pay the cost for the labor performed, and that someone is you. Anytime food has been cut, diced, sliced, juiced, shredded, trimmed, cooked, or processed, it will usually be more expensive (unless you have a few tricks in your rolled-up sleeves).

Dairy: Sliced or shredded cheese will cost more than a block of cheese. Some meat departments in larger markets keep a slicing machine just for cheese. I have asked them to slice my block of cheese for me at no extra charge. Otherwise, I slice or shred cheese myself.

Produce: Bags of precut salads will cost more than a head of lettuce. Select a vibrant head of green-leaf, red-leaf, or romaine lettuce (I've read many times that iceberg has no nutritional value and gums up your intestinal tract). Cut the lettuce yourself (I've also read that the admonition to *not* cut lettuce is based on myth)."Trimmed" broccoli and celery cost more than untrimmed. Use a potato peeler on broccoli stalks and slice them into medallions for stir-fry or salads. Lop the top off celery yourself and save it for soups. Red, green, and yellow peppers are expensive out of season. Buy them when they are plentiful, cut out the seed center, slice them into long strips, and freeze them in baggies for use year-round. I have done this for decades and do not bother to blanche before freezing.

Meat: Cut chicken will cost more than whole. The time, mess, and effort of cutting your own chicken, however, is a job that may not be worth the savings. I try to save an open afternoon to buy more than one chicken, lay several layers of plain brown paper bags on the counter, rinse the chicken, and hack away. I freeze baggies of legs, wings, breasts, and thighs. Everything else goes into an enormous pot with those celery tops, a bay leaf, and seasoning. After simmering for hours, I remove the chicken with a slotted spoon, which I then separate from the bones. All meat goes back into the broth, which I leave in the fridge overnight while the fat hardens. Once I discard the fat, I divvy the stock into several freezer containers and use it for soup, liquid to cook rice, or any recipe that calls for "broth."

Deli: Just about everything costs more in this department. I sometimes take a good, long look at salads sold in delis, especially in upscale markets. *Why, I can do that myself at home!* I reckon. And I do.

Floral: Arranged flowers cost more than cut flowers. I like to have fresh flowers around. Occasionally, we spring for a bouquet from the warehouse store. More often I just head outside. There are always wildflowers or branches that will bring a little creation indoors. I'm writing this in the fall, and I have long stalks of sedum mixed with red dogwood branches in four places in our home. Not only did I roll up my sleeves, I had the bonus of taking a walk in the fall colors, too!

Cereal: Instant oatmeal, especially in individual packages, is more expensive, and *way* less nutritional than whole cooked oats.

Juice: The more I read, the less inclined I am to encourage *anyone* to drink juice, organic or not, due to its glycemic index. Worse yet, juice *boxes*, while convenient, are far more costly than a can of frozen concentrate. In the case of children, this factors in a thermos for school, which factors in cleaning that thermos every night—actually a good chore for a child.

Seasonings: Seasoning packets are much more expensive than simply mixing a spice blend of your own. Besides, have you ever read the ingredients in those pre-packaged mixes? Yikes!

Doing It Yourself with Your Feet Up

Ever think of completing a task in front of the tube? Want to know what watching TV has to do with rolling up our sleeves? Stay tuned...

My husband and I watch TV. There are a couple of weekly shows we enjoy, and Joseph would surely perish without The Weather Channel. We are particularly interested in a design show, which we tape daily, because we are contemplating a downstairs makeover.

My point about doing something while watching TV is that it is a handy opportunity to accomplish some chores. My point is *not* that you should feel guilty if you simply watch TV.

■ After all my rant about not being fanatic, I confess that one of the things that drives me mad is wrinkled clothes. Rather than send Joseph's shirts to the cleaners, I iron while I watch TV. I also try to buy clothes that require little or no ironing. Permanent press, however, demands vigilance when drying clothes.

■ TV time is a perfect time to repair ripped seams, replace buttons, and iron patches on clothes. In my case, otherwise perfect jeans wear thin along the inner thigh. A non-abrasive patch ironed on the *inside* of the pant leg gives me at least another year's wear. I have ironed patches inside the knee of young children's pants.

■ I've used TV time to cross-stitch gifts, and I will probably begin a huge photo-sorting project watching the weather with Joe. Someday.

■ I've had manicures and pedicures in salons but simply cannot justify that expense. So I do them myself while watching my favorite show.

> *Hands:* We keep clippers, files, and lotion on an end table. We've learned that rough cuticles respond well to a dose of hand cream.

> *Feet: Ahhh…*I've whipped up a batch of foot scrub using kosher salt, olive oil, and lavender essential oil. I've also purchased one of those "foot rasps" because in my natural state I could grate potatoes on my heels. I lay down a big towel, prepare a tub of hot water, rasp away, rub foot scrub all over my feet, and soak. Quite a reduction in price from the "soaking" I would take in a salon!

■ In a perfect world I would exercise each morning. (I won't go into reality here.) I have, however, become adept with a beginner tape of an exercise regimen. Rather than watch the video, I've audio-taped the protocol. I exercise to my tape while I watch C-SPAN. I get two benefits in one: I do not pay dues to an athletic club and spend time and money driving there every day, and I hear lectures and interviews of political, historical, and cultural merit.

Smart Think:

People who say they can't probably don't.

Everyday Stuff

Doing it yourself is not about making entrance mats out of bottle tops or art deco out of plastic rings from your milk jugs. It's about facing the stuff of everyday care, maintenance, repair, and upgrade. At first try, your efforts to accomplish a task may seem awkward, expensive if you need equipment or tools, and a bit disappointing. But something happens the more you perform a certain task—it becomes second nature and your efficiency increases exponentially.

Cooking from Scratch

So let's take a drive through the arches, shall we?

After you pick up the kids from school, you decide to spend $12 for the three of you to eat. It's easier, and you are tired. But you have to drive five minutes out of your way to get to the restaurant.

Many other parents have the same idea, and the line is long, but you don't feel like parking and walking inside, so you fiddle with the steering wheel while the kids fuss in the back. By the time you get your food, 15 minutes have passed.

Add the five minutes out of your way to the normal trip home from school, and your drive home takes ten minutes.

Allow ten minutes to get everyone inside and the food unwrapped.

Forty minutes. And $12. On average. And you don't have *time* to cook from scratch? Or are you overwhelmed with the thought of going home and cooking real food? Let me share the meal I made last night, a meal that incorporated several of my principles: attitude, using things up, not wasting, creative genius, and rolling up my sleeves.

Staying at our son's home for the birth of our grandson, Benjamin, I opened the fridge and considered my possibilities: a huge amount of leftover chicken, one-half of an already-steamed spaghetti squash, about a cup of fresh spinach, a handful of mushrooms, and fresh broccoli. A big yam sat on the counter. Healthy food! Way to go, daughter-in-law!

In half the time it took the parent and children in my example to drive to the arches, I peeled, cubed, and microwaved the yam; cut small florets of broccoli and pared its stalks into medallions; scooped out the spaghetti squash and sautéed it in olive oil with the mushrooms and spinach; and cut the chicken into smallish pieces and sautéed them in tons of garlic, ginger, and olive oil.

Everyone was happily sated, and I felt positively flushed with satisfaction for the healthy meal I'd served my family. At their own table. Together.

> But as for you, be strong and do not give up, for your work will be rewarded.
>
> —2 CHRONICLES 15:7

CHAPTER 7

Use Things Up!

$\mathcal{I}$f I had to pick my favorite principle, "use things up" would receive serious consideration. This principle is intertwined with all the others. Just about any path I take ends up at the crossroads of "using" and "not wasting." (More on waste in the next chapter.)

This principle of using things appeals to me because it produces profound satisfaction and a sense of accomplishment. If you are intent on living on one income, pay close attention to this chapter and experience some pleasure yourself!

Consuming Is Consuming Us

I read a provocative article that pointed out we Americans live to consume, rather than consume to live. The magazine piece developed the observation that we are rampant consumers, spending and buying to fulfill some sort of psychological need, but we are not meeting that need. The percentage of Americans who say they are satisfied with their present financial situation dropped from 42 to 30 percent in recent years.

And so we tromp to the mall for recreation and wear sweatshirts emblazoned with "Shopping Diva." I admit it myself. When I am headed to my favorite bulk-foods store for a quarterly visit, I feel a rush of excitement and anticipation. Enough.

Just stop and look around you, right where you are. Study every single shelf, closet, and drawer. Peek inside the medicine cabinet and dump out your makeup case. If you are a man, wander into the garage or over to your workbench and take a gander at the tools you've amassed. (While you are at it, see if you can find my husband's pliers.) What is my point? *You bought most of the stuff you are looking at, toted it home, and put it down.* To take space.

Do you routinely wander around your house and put dollar bills on shelves? Of course not, you say! Oh, yes you do...

Even after you allow for things that must be kept for a specific application, for sentimental objects, or for seasonal items, take an honest look at the things you paid money for that just *sit*.

Vow to read the book, watch the video, use the makeup, the spices or exotic ingredients, finish the crochet or needlepoint, use the knife sharpener, jump on the exercise equipment, get excited once again over that hobby or craft. Make soups or stews that call for the tomatoes you canned last year, a strudel out of the pears. Replace the batteries in that toy or gadget and put it to work. Challenge yourself and use things up.

Apply simple logic: If you aren't using something anymore, give it to someone who will—and don't go out and buy that thing again. I am not suggesting you live threadbare and never shop again. That would be stupid. I am suggesting that you connect the dots and recognize how important stewarding your possessions is (more on *that* later). I end this admonition with a quote we have hanging in our home: "He who lives content with little has everything."

More logic: Don't buy a refill or a replacement until something is either empty or nearly empty (one would *not* want to wait to run out of certain things.) Time for a story.

The Adventures of ...YOU!

Making the mistake of watching an infomercial, you listened with rapt attention to the smart doctor as he convinced you that you could erase age marks and wrinkles if you bought a certain face cream. Never mind the doctor gets paid big bucks to hawk the cream, is really only an actor, or has a stake in the company. Having wrinkles yourself, you dropped everything and drove 25 miles into town, raced into the most expensive natural foods store in a 200-mile radius, and sure enough, they had the cream. Down you plunked your credit card, out you ran to the car, back home you sped.

You seem to remember a protocol for using that cream, but you got lazy. It ended up in your bathroom drawer alongside several other tubes, jars, and tins of face creams guaranteed to get rid of age spots and wrinkles.

> *Smart Think:*
>
> **Did I bring that thing home to occupy space?**

Look Around You

If you are determined to save money, two of the most rewarding habits you can develop are *knowing* what you have (organization) and *using* what you have. Walk through your house. Look in your closets, in your drawers, and on your shelves. Discover things that should be used or could be used up.

Do you see books, furniture, clothes, groceries, gadgets, exercise equipment, musical instruments, magazines, makeup, crafts, games, and perfectly good bubble bath going to waste?

Explore the garage, the basement, the storage unit and ponder: *Will I really and truly use that set of bocce balls, the horseshoes, the camping gear...?*

A Note on Storage Units

Just how much is that storage unit costing you each month, anyway?

Some people have good reason to rent a storage unit—for a time. If you are renting one merely to stash the overflow from your house, maybe you have too much stuff.

Bonus

The bonus built into this principle is that by using what you have, you spent your money wisely.

What do you already have that you can use today, tomorrow, or next month in lieu of spending money? This chapter is dedicated to finding some of those things and offering suggestions for their use. Our first stop as we begin to explore your home is that treasure trove we call the kitchen. You do realize, don't you, that most of you could feed your family for *weeks* by simply using what you already have...

Become a Kitchen Magician

Unless you are preparing for a political or natural disaster, another way to say "Use things in the kitchen" is, "Don't hoard food."

We've already discussed the compulsive ritual we go through each week called "grocery shopping." Why do we trudge to the store week after week, bring things home, and put them away, never to be seen, used, or eaten? Just as renting a storage unit for overflow from your home means you have too much stuff, cramming cupboards so full that cans topple and boxes crumble means you have enough groceries already.

Some of the greatest meals we have in our home are built around something in the fridge that is getting "long in the tooth" or something performing a sit-in on the pantry shelf.

Use things up! Don't hoard! Sip!

Tea Time!

Sip? Sure! Why not start your trip through the kitchen with a cup of tea? The simple act of taking tea calms us down, brings beauty into our day, and evokes a feeling of rest. Tea soothes and adds a touch of civility to harried lives. Tea can be social or solitary, robust or gentle, invigorating or calming. Tea is a private retreat, a Brahms' lullaby, an encounter with our inside world while we leave the outside world behind.

Close your eyes and put your senses on autopilot as you sit back after a sip of tea and contemplate the mystery—of why we let our tea go stale and languish, stuffed in half-opened boxes jammed back behind the box of instant mashed potatoes. Or shoved into a jar on our kitchen counter.

Here's a simple project: Separate your tea collection by type: herb, black, green, blended. Gather pretty tins and labels for each tea type. Buy sugar cubes to store in an old-fashioned sugar bowl. Scout your cupboards for teacups. Make simple scones, call up your friends, and have a tea party. As a bonus...

1. You finally used some of your tea.

2. You organized your world and made it prettier.

3. You creatively did something different.

4. You saved money by having an easy, inexpensive "party."

Tea-rrific Idea!

Brew your own blend by mixing teas you have or by adding spice or dried fruit to the teapot. Experiment until you have your very own concoction. Limit yourself to ingredients on hand. Use cloves, tiny chunks of cinnamon stick, or curls of dried lemon peel or orange peel. (No, not the stuff you cleaned out from under the kitchen sink.) Add fresh or dried mint leaves. Who knows? You may concoct a brew so tasty that it will become your "signature" gift during the holidays.

Freezer Burn

Let's revisit our old friend, the Fort Knox of your home, that cosmic hole called the freezer. We've already talked about organizing the freezer. If you haven't yet met that challenge, what happens now when you open the freezer door? Allow me.

You open the freezer, shove something in, and slam the door quickly—before last year's meat loaf falls on your foot.

Reach in for ice cubes and you find the tray empty. Fold the lid back on your craving for Rocky Road and peer into a mass of icky-tasting ice crystals.

While the refrigerator is home to our latest science project, we create modern art in the freezer, as chunks of frozen meat, veggies, and pizza parts weld together with sticky goo from leaking juice cans. Could it be that this is one place where we stash things and forget about them because it is so c-c-c...cold? Wear gloves when entering!

Tip: Knowing what you have and using it is not only frugal, it also keeps frozen foods from degrading in quality and nutritive value. Most meats, for instance, can be stored in the freezer up to nine months. Since it has so much surface, however, hamburger has an average freezer life of three months. (Freezer-burned foods are best "hidden" in soups or stews.)

Project: Try to live off your freezer one week at a time. As a bonus...

1. You will discover the pot roast that's been buried under an avalanche of ice cream and frozen pot pies.

2. Your family will be glad you finally cooked the roast.

Don't Forget the Kitchen Sink

This is also something we talked about in the organization chapter. If I were an oddsmaker, I'd bet that nine out of ten of us have duplicate cleaning supplies under the kitchen sink right now. Use them up. And then develop a close association with the people down at the janitorial supply shop. Get so chummy they invite you to their son's bar mitzvah. (The "cleaning" aisle in the supermarket will clean out your wallet quicker than a squeegee on a wet windowpane.)

Project: Vow to consolidate cleaning products (I'm thinking of that blue window-washing spray, for starters) and not spring for a "new and improved" brand until a refill is necessary. Then introduce yourself to the janitorial supply folks. As a bonus...

1. You will become an ace at cleaning because you have the proper supplies and because of the advice you received from your new friends at the janitorial supply store.

2. You will never again buy those messy, sudsy cleaning pads that rust and fall apart.

3. The space under your kitchen sink will no longer look like the aftermath of a frat party.

The Spice of Life

Cats have nine lives. Herbs and spices do not. Sprinkle, shake, or *dump,* and create a masterpiece for dinner tonight.

The shelf life for most herbs is one year; for spices, it's two years. If in doubt, smell. If you can't smell anything, rub the herbs between your fingers to activate the oils. If you still don't smell anything, spice up the compost pile. Some spices store well in the fridge, others (such as vanilla) do not. Do not store any spices or herbs near heat or light.

Tip: Shopping in a health food store or bulk product store takes a lot of consumer savvy. However, you should always buy herbs and spices in bulk. Prices for those small jars in supermarkets are out of sight! The warehouse stores peddle spices in five-gallon buckets! What to do? If you need only a bit of something for a particular recipe, *buy only that amount*—in bulk. As a bonus…

1. Proper storage maximizes your investment in herbs and spices.

2. Once you learn the shelf life of perishables, you will be inclined to use them before they degrade.

3. You will be less inclined to spend money on a larger quantity of *anything* perishable once you become aware of the shelf life of most items.

4. You can use some of those rusty pennies from your medicine cabinet to pay the tiny amount due when you buy in bulk.

Spice Up Your Life

What exactly is a spice, anyway? Spices are mainly dried seeds, roots, or stems of tropical plants. What do you *do* with them? Here are some suggestions.

- Use cardamom in coffee cakes, chicken curry, and coffee. Try peeling, coring, and slicing some apples. Sauté them in butter and sprinkle them with powdered cardamom.

- Use celery seed in soups, stews, eggs, spaghetti sauce (honest), potato salad, and any vegetable dish.

- Use cinnamon in baking, on toast, on sweet potatoes, in yogurt, and on rice. You could even brew it for a pleasing scent in your home.

- Use cloves in gingerbread or on ham, stick whole ones in an onion for flavor, or put them in an orange for a holiday pomander ball.

- Use coriander in salsas, beans, Middle-Eastern dishes. Know what fresh coriander is called? Cilantro.

- Use cumin in soups, curries, chilies, and dips.

- Use ginger in baking, tea, fish, soup, and stir fry.

- Use nutmeg in baking, in meat sauces, and on yogurt.

- Use paprika in salads, on eggs, in goulash, and in chicken dishes.

- Use pepper on top of just about everything but baked goods (unless you're making pepper cookies). Fresh-ground is best.

Give Thanks All Year 'Round

Is there a kitchen in the Northern Hemisphere that does not have a can of pumpkin in the cupboard? Make pumpkin pie. (One survey claimed that pumpkin pie aroma sent men swooning—it's more powerful than eau de parfum.) Don't want to make pie? Make bread. Or muffins. Or soup. Need a recipe? Reach for one of your several hundred thousand cookbooks.

Project: Find a recipe for pumpkin soup. As a bonus...

1. You get tons of carotene.

2. You've "colored" outside the lines.

Can't Cook Without a Book!

Ever meet a cookbook you didn't want? I bet you bought a bunch you didn't *use!* Who can resist the fabulous food shots on the covers of the cookbook that's piled high on the bargain rack at the bookstore? We *all* dream of new recipes that will transport us to distant lands and land us acclaim from friends and family.

And the assortment! A cookbook for every country on the planet, a cookbook for every *planet!,* one for every food group, one for every diet, even one for every body type. Preparing the recipes from every book would take three lifetimes. *That's okay,* you say to yourself, *I've got the time.* Right on!

Project: Pick a favorite cookbook from your sagging shelf. Make a hobby out of preparing every recipe in that book. Write comments in the margins. Keep a backup pizza in the freezer just in case. As a bonus...

1. You will expand your culinary talents.

2. Both you and your family will have a lot of fun.

3. You will have a new hobby.

4. You will eat pizza every now and then.

Leftovers

What's for lunch? Dinner! We believe in leftovers in our house. Leftovers cut down on effort, time spent cooking, and energy consumption. In the Yates' perfect world, dinner tonight is lunch tomorrow. Either Joe or I prepare enough extra food to guarantee leftovers. When the leftovers have cooled, we put them into containers, then into Joe's lunch box (when I can get him to bring it in), then into the fridge. In the morning, he grabs and goes. We also freeze leftovers as future meals. This works well with soups and stews.

Project: Turn to one of those unused cookbooks for a chili recipe. Make a double batch. Have chili and cornbread for dinner, and label and freeze the rest.

Tip: Labeling what you put into the freezer is vital. (I once made a smoothie from frozen fish stock. Yum.) As a bonus...

1. At least once in the next month or so you will have only to heat some chili and serve it with rolled tortillas.

2. You will have something on hand for a neighbor or friend in need.

3. You will have something on hand for impromptu visitors.

Don't Put That Cookbook Away!

"Lettuce" say you have romaine in your fridge that needs to be used...*fast!* Look under "lettuce" or "salad" in the index of your cookbooks and find a recipe you can make with whatever else is on hand. I have practiced this with perishables for years and have discovered some tasty new recipes. The same method could be used for anything in the kitchen that has been there too long. Why not build an entire meal around the wild rice, the half box of wheat crackers, or the jar of pesto.

Tip: Don't pick a recipe that requires you to shop for needed ingredients.

Project: Go to your fridge right now. I'll wait. Determine which perishable is having a near-death experience. Is it sour cream, something left over, sandwich meat, cheese? Maybe a couple of shriveled kiwi? Find a way to save it (freeze) or use it. As a bonus…

1. You may think twice before you buy such a big container of sour cream again.

2. You will learn how to peel kiwi. (With a potato peeler.)

3. You will dazzle your friends with Dead Cheese Pie.

Dead Cheese Pie

Kids love this! It uses up that old cheese you have in your refrigerator. It's even great in the lunch box.

Ingredients

2 cups cooked spaghetti

1–2 tablespoons melted butter or olive oil

2 tablespoons dry parsley

1/2 cup chopped onion

4–6 eggs

about 2 cups old cheese, crumbled or shredded

salt and pepper

Heat butter or olive oil, sauté onions and parsley, let cool a bit. Beat eggs in a bowl and add some of the cheese. Mix everything together and spread into 9" by 9" pan. Bake 25 minutes at 350 degrees. Cut into squares.

The Adventures of Frugal Woman

I read that oysters really and truly are aphrodisiacs in a sense because they are so high in zinc, and *none* of us gets enough zinc, for heaven's sake. So I bought a quart of shucked, raw oysters, planning, of course, to dole out a couple to Wonder Man every day, my way of revving up his engine, so to speak. Well, shucks is right!

Wonder Man got called out of town for a few weeks. And there was the matter of that pesky expiration date.

"*How* many oysters did you eat?!" my doctor said in dismay.

$\sim$ $\sim$ $\sim$

Check Shelf Life Dates

- *Expiration date* or *use by* means the last day the product should be used.

- *Sell by* means the last day the product can be sold, allowing time to be stored and used at home.

- *Best if used by* means that after this date the product may be safe but not at peak quality.

Use It or Lose It

Are you using the juicer? The espresso maker? The ice cream maker? The waffle iron? If not, will you?

Agreed, many of these things came as gifts, and parting with things that friends or family members gave you is hard—especially because they paid *their* hard-earned cash for them. And for sure, you've used some appliances for a little while, but the effort was too much, the interest waned, or you simply do not eat waffles anymore. If you have tired of an appliance, or find it too cumbersome to use, use it or lose it.

Tip: One reason small appliances are not used is that we cannot easily access them in the kitchen. Understandably, they get shoved way back on the bottom shelf of some cabinet, or buried under a heap of baking tins and plastic grocery bags. If you are inclined to use an appliance regularly, build a "garage" for it on your counter (ready-made at some home improvement stores), or keep it in an accessible spot in a nearby room. If, for instance, you don't pop corn often, but *do* intend to pop corn (especially for those awesome popcorn balls of yours at Christmas), keep the popcorn popper on a shelf downstairs.

Project: Evaluate every one of your "handy" appliances. If you honestly will not use it, then donate it, give it away, or sell it at a yard sale. As a bonus...

1. You will have lots more room in the kitchen.

2. You will be less dependent on electricity.

3. You might get into this idea and apply the same philosophy to baking equipment, pots and pans, and that abundant collection of gizmos and gadgets in your kitchen drawer.

Bonanzas in the Bedroom

Does anything go unused in the bedroom besides the platoon of perfume and aftershave on your dressers? Who ever said that dusty, capless perfume bottles, clustered on dusty, mirrored trays, are *de rigueur* in bedroom decor? Like spices, perfumes lose their quality in about a year. So say the experts. Drizzle some in your bathwater if you have to! Do something!

Project: Put one bottle of perfume on your nightstand. Every evening before bed, spritz some gently into the room. As a bonus...

1. It's not pumpkin pie, but who knows...

2. You'll enjoy a pleasant aroma as you nod off to sleep.

The Adventures of Frugal Woman

During one of my household "sweeps," I found midnight blue satin sheets in a basement box. To the thrift store, or to use? No question! Always wanting to rev up our love life, I decided this would be a night to remember. Upstairs I raced. Pillows flying, blankets on the floor, I wrapped the bed in blue. Candles came from all around the house, perfume was spritzed, and I slinked into a nifty satin nightgown. No matter the long sleeves and that it hung just below my knees; Wonder Man would be dazzled.

"I'm coming, Wonder Man!" I yelled. And in a playful mood I ran into the bedroom and dove onto the bed. Satin on satin makes for pretty poor friction. I hit the wall at 45 MPH. We thought twice before we went to the emergency room.

~ ~ ~

Dump Out the Jewelry Box

You might very well have costume jewelry from the 60s in your jewelry box. Or a pinky ring that went the way of the Edsel. The last time I looked, I had a picture from my junior prom and a button that said "Kiss me, I'm Polish." I kept the picture but kissed the button good-bye.

Project: Make a fun gift for your daughter, granddaughter, or niece. Line a simple wooden box with a scrap of velvet. Plop all that costume jewelry inside. Big, ugly rings will score particularly high. Sell the pinky ring for its gold. (*Careful!* Don't give anything that has either a pin or choking potential to a small child.) As a bonus…

1. This is a low-cost gift that will be treasured and *used*.

2. You got rid of a bunch of junk.

3. Getting rid of a bunch of junk made you think about how much money you have spent on junk. Not to mention how goofy you must have looked with those big papier mâché, dangling, day-glow pink earrings.

4. If you have good pieces of jewelry that you don't use, turn them into heirlooms and pass them on.

Belt It!

Challenge yourself to create one brand-new, dynamite outfit by mixing and matching things you already have. A change in the way you look on the outside can often have a dramatic effect on how you feel on the inside. A nip, a tuck, a different color, or abandoning a particular piece of clothing that has not only become your identity but your security blanket of sorts, may delight and surprise you. (My security blanket? Black turtle-necks.)

Project: Surprise everyone and change your look. Put a belt on a beltless outfit. Change the belt you normally wear. Sport a vest—or take one off. As a bonus...

1. Once you're adept at mixing and matching, you will become more particular when you buy new clothes. They will have to mix...or match!

2. You will surprise yourself with the dress-up potential you now have.

3. You will learn which styles and colors bring out your rugged good looks or your stunning beauty.

I'm Not Making This Up

Alrighty then. Shall we talk makeup? Foundation has a shelf life, too. The oils in foundation can turn rancid. Old mascara can be a bacteria factory. And glitter eye shadow somehow doesn't work well on a 55-year-old who is starting to get about as wrinkled as an old kiwi. That white lipstick you've kept all these years? That red lipstick you bought when you were trying to "look your age?" Fah-get about it!

Project: Some stuff you just have to throw out. As a bonus...

1. Your skin will thank you.

Recommended Daily Allowance: Zero

That's about it—zero nutritional value if you don't take those vitamins you once *ran* out to buy and that now occupy space. Let me guess: They are either on the windowsill above the kitchen sink, huddled in a corner on your counter, or heaped in piles on shelves. I know...you read a book or a magazine article that convinced you a particular supplement was just the ticket for ditching the flu, for beating some disease at its game, or for more energy. (Remember the oysters?)

Whether you should take vitamin supplements isn't for me to say. What I want to say is what I've been saying for several pages: You spent money for that stuff.

Tip: You might be wise to investigate *proper times of day* to take certain supplements. While you are at it, learn which vitamins go well together, which ones should be kept separate, and which ones work best with food. (Dr. Sidney Baker wrote a book called *The Circadian Prescription* [Putnam Publishing Group, 2000], in which he discusses such things.)

Project: Delegate a small pudding dish for each person on a vitamin protocol. Label dishes with names. Sort daily vitamins into each person's dish and swallow away. As a bonus...

1. You may find out if the claims about a vitamin's miraculous power were true.

2. You may feel better because you are being proactive toward better health.

3. No more lineup on the windowsill.

Move the Couch!

Rearrange your furniture for a fresh, less-cluttered look. Try to create clusters of furniture for seating arrangement and design. Don't line your furniture all around the room. A change, however slight, energizes us and puts a little bit of zest in our lives. (More on this in the Presentation chapter.)

Project: Take away a few pieces of furniture and streamline your living room. Accent with throw pillows (knew those pillows would show up sooner or later...), area rugs, or afghans. As a bonus...

1. You redecorate your home with what you already have.

2. You give your spirits a boost by changing things.

3. You clean behind the couch.

Or Add a Dresser

Haul an old dresser from the basement to the living room, bathroom, or kitchen. Use it for storage or as a centerpiece. "Primitive" or distressed furniture is all the rage. My bathroom sink rests in a big wooden bureau with a hole bored in it.

Project: You will be astonished at the change you can make if you just move furniture around from room to room. As a bonus...

1. You will create new storage space.

2. You will discover your creative genius (an entire chapter on that is ahead).

3. You will be astonished.

Theme Party!

You just might have found your favorite video when you moved your couch. Rewind the video and host a theme party. Ask your guests to wear "theme" costumes and bring a potluck "theme" dish. We have thrown a "Black Stallion" party to rave reviews. One old-timer came as a beatnik, because "that's the way he dressed back then."

Project: Have a "Winnie the Pooh" night. Dress like Christopher Robin and serve honey cakes. Host a "Gone With the Wind" party, dress like Scarlet and Rhett, and eat pecan pie. As a bonus...

1. This is entertainment on a shoestring.

2. Everyone contributes to the meal.

3. You get to see what your friends look like dressed like Piglet and Pooh.

Table This Idea

So where *are* all of your pretty tablecloths? What about that lace beauty Gram gave you from her prized collection? What about the gorgeous holiday runner you picked up for a song?

Project: Round up all of your tablecloths. Dig into the unkempt piles in the linen closet and pull them out. Iron any serious wrinkles. Fold the tablecloths lengthwise and drape them over sturdy clothes hangers. Now find some space in one of your closets and hang your tablecloths all in a row. As a bonus...

1. Your tablecloths will be immediately accessible.

2. You will be able to see all tablecloths at once and pick the color, style, and "theme" for your meal.

3. You will feel terrific when you clear the table and cover it with a pretty cloth.

4. For the first time in your life, your friends will think you are some sort of "neat-freak"...something you *never* thought you'd hear!

Alleluia, Tra La La

Play the praise tape you once bought. Let the melody of praise pulse through your home in thanksgiving for the blessings the Lord bestows upon you: the sun, the stars, the gift of friends and family, and your one income. As a matter of fact, play *all* the tapes and CDs you bought once upon a time.

Project: Dance around your house with the joy that King David felt. As a bonus...

1. Dreary days will become less so.

2. Psalm 150 tells us to praise God with tambourine and dance. (But don't jump on the furniture. I did once and broke a couch.)

3. You might be less inclined to buy a tape or CD if you listen to what you already have.

4. Your heavenly Father just might tap His toe and smile back.

Floral Design for Peanuts

What on earth are we to do with those Styrofoam "peanuts" that are used for packing?

Project: Use packing peanuts instead of rocks or pebbles for drainage under potted plants. As a bonus...

1. You will rest your back, not having to lift Arnold Schwartzen-petunia.

Filling the Subscription—Twice

Save a favorite magazine for one year. Bundle the issues with raffia and give them to a friend.

Project: Tie a whisk or dowel rolling pin on top of cooking magazines. If you're giving fashion magazines, wrap them with that scarf you never wore. If you're giving travel magazines, include a compass or a map. If it's sporting magazines, include some fishing lures. As a bonus...

1. You get twice as much for your investment.

2. This is a low-cost gift you can present with pizzazz.

3. You've joined the recycle bunch.

Ideas for Using Some Food Items

▪ Leftover snacks magically disappear! Keep putting what's left into smaller bowls. This is an important trick for all food service. When the bowl *looks* full, it becomes inviting. A handful of chips at the bottom of a big bowl? Unappetizing.

▪ Do you have leftover ketchup in a nearly empty bottle? Add oil and vinegar, and give a shake. Salad dressing.

▪ Is some oatmeal languishing on a shelf?

1. Use oatmeal browned in butter as a substitute for nuts.

2. Use oatmeal instead of bread crumbs.

3. Use oatmeal in meatloaf.

▪ Warm lemons before squeezing and they will yield almost twice as much juice.

▪ Declare a Use Things Up Week in your home. Build meals out of food that has been sitting around. Get silly with the kids. Tell them to create a culinary master-piece with an old can of chocolate syrup or with a box of macaroni and cheese.

Since God has mercies to give, and He intends to give them to us, those mercies are not broken pieces or someone else's leftovers...God has bags that were never untied, never opened up, but set aside through a thousand generations for those who hope in His mercy.

—JOHN BUNYAN

CHAPTER 8

Waste Not

What Is the Matter with Us?

We've talked about developing savvy in order to survive on one income; we've talked about organization; we've talked about "do it yourself" and using what we have. Now we are ready to talk about throwing our money out the window—and, by example, teaching our children to do the same. We are ready to talk about waste.

Let me get right to the point: Do you throw food in the garbage?

Do you realize that when we waste, we rob from the backs and steal from the mouths of others? When we waste, we shamefully ignore the poverty and hunger of the disenfranchised.

Hold on! Do you mean to say that if Missy doesn't eat her peas I'm contributing to world hunger? Now just wait a minute...

That is exactly what I am saying, but (here comes the broken record) I never want to sound fanatic. I do not mean to use His name flippantly, but God knows how hard we try to get young children to eat their food. Some food is surely going to go to waste. (Advantage—cocker spaniel.) Yet as stern as this sounds, you need not allow your children to waste. Teach them now. I believe with all of my heart that we insult every hungry person on this planet when we are careless with food. The old ploy our parents used about eating our bread crust because "someone was starving in China" became the butt of jokes, but that message has merit and is not at all funny.

When we waste, we also dishonor God and the blessings He has given us. How do you think He feels as we squander our abundance?

The good news is that you, and many like you, want to achieve sensible balance in your view toward consumption. If you didn't, you wouldn't be holding this book right now. Thank you for your commitment to a more meaningful set of values.

In July of 1995, a report revealed that many people like you...

1.   regret that materialism dominates their lives

2.   are alarmed about the future

3.   see a connection between their way of life and the environment

4.   are torn between two earnest desires

   ■   On one hand, we all strive toward financial security and material comfort.

   ■   On the other hand, our deepest aspirations tend to be nonmaterial.

How Are We Perceived?

Having a son who is a sociologist can be unsettling. Through his studies, I have learned how we Americans are perceived by others in the world: not very well.

Smart Think:

What is the real inflation in this country? Could it be our "inflated" needs and perceived desires?

This seems like a real conundrum. Just about everything we do is imitated as "the good life" by people around the world as America sets the standard for global consumption. On the flip side, we are viewed as a country of excess, caricatured as fat and lazy, with fat and lazy children. This opinion is tragic. It is tragic not only because we have fostered this image but also because our might and our Christian convictions *carry a responsibility toward others*. Nearly 80 percent of Americans identify themselves as Christians. Christians follow Jesus Christ. What did our Master tell us about caring for others? Shouldn't the world see an image of Christ when they look our way? After all, 80 percent is a whole lot of people.

> *Smart Think:*
>
> How can I share my blessings with others today?

Stewardship

As I've commented, our sovereign God has blessed some of us with material and financial security. We should not be ashamed of that. Think of the consequence if everyone who was "rich" liquidated and joined the ranks of the poor! When Jesus told the rich young ruler to sell all, He was not giving us a general mandate. He was speaking to the rich young ruler. One of the reasons God allows some to be wealthy is that He uses that wealth toward the betterment of His kingdom. We should honor Him through responsible stewardship of whatever He has bestowed.

All of our earthly goods ultimately come from God and belong to Him. Psalm 68:19 (NKJV) joyfully proclaims: "Blessed be the Lord, who daily loads us with benefits, the God of our salvation!" We manage those benefits on His behalf. Our level of responsibility in His eternal kingdom will depend on how we manage the resources that God has given us in this life. This includes our attitude and Christian witness as we manage our financial affairs.

Any other outlook leads to a divided mind. We can't serve God if we are convinced that our money and property belong to us. We will inevitably end up serving them. "No one can serve two masters," said Jesus. "Either he will hate the one and love the other, or he will be devoted to the one and despise the other. You cannot serve both God and money" (Matthew 6:24).

Should We All Be Poor?

Good question! If we consider the disenfranchised in so many parts of the world, we are rich beyond their wildest dreams. Yet when we consider those who live in luxury, we ourselves seem poor. The issue is not whether we are rich or poor but rather that which we talked about in chapter 2—our attitude. What is our attitude to be?

In 1 Timothy 6:6-10, the apostle Paul gives us a pretty good idea:

> But godliness with contentment is great gain. For we brought nothing into the world, and we can take nothing out of it. But if we have food and clothing, we will be content with that. People who want to get rich fall into temptation and a trap and into many foolish and harmful desires that plunge men into ruin and destruction. For the love of money is a root of all kinds of evil.

Paul goes on to instruct his protégé, Timothy:

> Command those who are rich in this present world not to be arrogant nor to put their hope in wealth, which is so uncertain, but to put their hope in God, who richly provides us with everything for our enjoyment. Command them to do good, to be rich in good deeds, and to be generous and willing to share. In this way they will lay up treasure for themselves as a firm foundation for the coming age, so that they may take hold of the life that is truly life (verses 17-19).

The Adventures of Frugal Woman's Sister

My sister had to clean a basement at her business that was filled with trash: mildewed mattresses, pop bottles...stuff that was earmarked for the local landfill. She sheepishly called someone who is an advocate for a small community of elderly Russian women in her town, women who had escaped religious persecution.

My sister called because she thought the women might want something in that mess downstairs. A few hours later, she stood in complete embarrassment as an old Pinto station wagon sagged under the weight of everything in the basement...*everything*.

An old Russian woman with a babushka on her head rolled down the window of the car, and with tears in her eyes grasped my sister's hand and said: "Thank you, thank you! Now I am a rich woman."

~ ~ ~

A Word About Our Gifts

God has blessed us with more than material or financial assets. He has blessed each of us with talents and gifts that are unique to us alone. Some households choose to live on one income specifically so they can better steward these gifts. And whether you tithe from your income or not, God does not want 10 percent from us—He wants all of us. In His service. To His glory.

Read the parable of the talents in Matthew 25. What does the parable mean to us? We are given gifts so that others will profit from them. The bottom line is this...

Smart Think:

~

Do I determine my value by what I have?

~

- If you can sing, are you singing?

- If you can laugh, are you bringing joy to a melancholy world?

- If you can extend your hand, are you reaching to a stranger in need?

- If you can write, are you writing?

A man should always consider how much he has more than he wants, and how much more unhappy he might be than he really is.

—Joseph Addison

What Is Your Waste Quotient?

1. Do I throw food in the garbage?

2. Why do I throw food in the garbage?

3. What can I do to stop throwing food in the garbage?

4. What will I waste during the next holiday season?

5. What can I do to curtail that waste?

6. Am I wasting the talents and gifts that God has graced me with?

7. Am I sensibly recycling?

8. Am I wasting some of God's splendid creation by not enjoying a sunset, a walk in the woods, and the sound of birds?

9. Am I wasting resources?

10. Am I honoring God through sensible stewardship?

The Food Problem

I'm told that if everyone in America threw away one tablespoon of cranberry sauce on Thanksgiving Day, that amount would equal *6 million pounds*. Quite an eye-opener, isn't it? Most of us are concerned about wasting food; many of us recognize that people in China and elsewhere are, indeed, starving. We don't want to throw food in the trash. But how do we fight rot in the veggie bin or get the kids to stop flinging their food at the spaniel?

If you scrape half-filled plates into the trash after each meal, are you serving food your family will not eat? Could it be you serve too much food? Or are you hopelessly butting heads with the finicky eater in the family? Parenting experts certainly offer advice about the care and feeding of Missy and Junior. (Josh would not eat raw tomatoes or squash in any form when he was a youngster. We honored that and didn't force the issue.)

If eliminating waste is not practical, can you make use of the food otherwise? Freeze it for later use? Collect leftovers for soup, stir-fry, or stew? Scrape them into the dog dish? Put the waste on the compost pile? (Incidentally, trees love coffee grounds and milk that has soured.)

Three Suggestions for Children Who Are Finicky Eaters

1. Presentation boils down to how you prepare and present the meal.

2. Ownership means including children in food selection and preparation.

3. Patience means they will eat when they get hungry. Honest.

Food Storage

What does storage have to do with spending money? Everything! Why be judicious in spending money if you lose your savings through neglect, rot, or decay? Proper storage of food is a critical aspect of smart living.

Besides refrigerating, we can store food in three ways: canning, dehydrating, and freezing.

Times are changing. Not many people can from their veggie gardens any longer. Frankly, the nutritional quality of home-canned produce is coming into question. I have been an avid canner for decades, but I am opting more and more for dehydration and freezing.

Dehydrating, however, is simply not on everyone's top-ten list of things to do on a Saturday afternoon, so that leaves freezing.

I freeze just about everything: leftovers, homemade stock, meat from a great sale, and fish from a fisher friend. Among other things, I keep extra coffee beans in the freezer, well-wrapped paint brushes if I am in the midst of a painting job, and a sack of peas as a cold pack for medical emergencies.

If you freeze, wrap food properly to keep out air, and label, label, label, including the date. Remember my fish milk shake? The cats thought it was terrific.

Some stores donate expired food to a food rescue program or a homeless shelter, some don't. I once bought *buckets* of fresh herbs past their expiration date for $2. They were on their way to the dumpster. Ask the store produce manager what he does with expired merchandise. You may have to bring things home and roll up your sleeves—*fast*—but you've saved money and saved the waste of that food.

The Adventures of Frugal Woman

This one was over the top—literally. And I blame it all on my mother. *She's* the one who planted the notion that I must never, ever waste. And that it was my bounden duty to prevent waste anywhere I encountered it. This encounter took place at a local dumpster.

Helping us find boxes to pack our household for the eight-mile trip to our new digs, a friend of our son's accompanied me to our local market. Imagine our chagrin when we discovered a dumpster behind the market with sides six feet high.

"Boost me up," I said to Glenn, who obliged to the best of his ability. Fingers laced together, the poor lad hoisted me by my feet until I was waist high with the edge of the dumpster. I immediately lost focus of our mission.

"There are bags and bags of croutons in here!" I yelled, draping my body over the dumpster's edge, my ample posterior protruding like a rocky crag on the Oregon coast.

"Mrs. Yates!" came the cry of astonishment from below as bag after bag rained down on the hapless lad like fireworks on the Fourth of July.

"Oh my word, there are packages of stir-fry veggies in here!" I exclaimed, just before I fell in. (Yes, I left them in the dumpster.)

~ ~ ~

Basic Storage Supplies

Have on hand a sensible supply of jars, tins, labels, food storage bags, freezer bags and paper, markers, masking tape, and clothespins. *Clothespins?* Yes! Once you use them in place of twist ties to close plastic storage bags, you will wonder how you lived without them.

Produce

If you get to know *anyone* in your supermarket, get to know your produce manager. That person will lead you to the freshest and most economical buy in the department. That person will also answer your questions about proper storage.

Hardly any of us had training in produce care. We have learned by trial and error, learned from our mothers, or not really learned at all.

All produce requires proper care for safe and sensible keeping as well as for freshness and vitality. Grocers have a protocol called the "Produce Life Support System" (I kid you not). Once produce is picked from its source, it begins gradual deterioration. Each item requires proper storage conditions to prolong its useful life. (Don't laugh, this is important.)

All produce breathes in carbon dioxide and breathes out oxygen and a gas called ethylene. There are six elements involved in proper produce care:

Respiration: This is the most important thing for you to know. The faster the produce breathes, the faster it ripens, and the shorter the shelf life. Fast breathers must be slowed down to ensure quality. Strawberries, for instance, breathe ten times faster at 70 degrees than at 33 degrees.

Temperature: Fast breathers are stored in cold temperatures to make them slow down. Excessive chilling, however, is counterproductive, causing starches to convert to sugars, which leads to decay. Avocados, for instance, turn black inside when kept at lower than 45 degrees.

Water: Did you know that most plants are 90 to 95 percent water? No wonder we eat them when dieting! We have vegetable crispers in our refrigerators to help conserve water. Some vegetables, such as asparagus, are no different from cut flowers in their need for water. Droopy produce is not always too old to use. Many times it can be refreshed in a bath of warm water. Soak it in lukewarm water for ten minutes, dry it, then put it in the fridge for a while. Presto!

Air circulation: This is critical because plants must continue breathing. If too much ethylene accumulates, you have decay. Remove tight-fitting covers or wrappers and replace with loose bags when you store. Carrots must be stored in bags with holes because carrots emit a gas that causes a bitter taste.

Light: Light stimulates photosynthesis, which is why potatoes should be covered. They turn green if stored in excessive light. And you all know what green potatoes can do!

Odor control: Produce quickly absorbs the air around it, so unusual flavors will develop when bad odors are present. Put a strawberry next to an onion and you are going to have mighty strange-tasting shortcake! Fresh mushrooms are magnets to just about any odor in the area and should be stored in a loosely-closed brown paper bag in the fridge.

Produce Respiration Table

(Betcha this is the first book you ever bought with this in it.)

Extremely high (refrigerate ASAP): berries, lima beans, avocados, mushrooms, corn, asparagus, peas, broccoli, spinach

Very high: green beans, artichokes, Brussels sprouts

Moderate: apricots, bananas, cherries, peaches, nectarines, celery, plums, figs, new potatoes, tomatoes, peppers, carrots, cabbage

Slow: apples, citrus fruits, grapes, kiwi, garlic, onions, mature potatoes, sweet potatoes

Very slow: nuts, dates, dried fruits

Tip: Because some nuts may go rancid, it's always better to err on the safe side and store them in the fridge.

Do not store tomatoes in the fridge unless *very* ripe. Never store potatoes in the fridge (makes the inside turn black). The fridge dries out most breads.

Bananas Getting Ripe Too Fast?

- Stick them in the freezer, right in their skins. Use at a later date to make bread, muffins, smoothies. (Skin them first.)

- Mash them first and put them in baggies in the freezer for later use.

- We get up to one week more from our bananas if we refrigerate them when they begin to get too ripe. The skin turns black but the inside is fine.

Keeping the Moths Out: Clothing Care

In the same way that proper food storage can stretch our grocery dollars, care and repair of our clothing can keep us looking good for less.

We live in such a disposable society that we think nothing of replacing everything we own over and over. In addition, Madison Avenue has convinced us we aren't normal unless we dress the same as everyone else. Phooey! Quality clothes with a classic look will last a lifetime.

Here are some tips that will help keep that classic look looking classy:

- Take permanent press items out of the dryer at once.

- Don't use wire hangers for heavy clothing.

- Clothes last longer if they are kept out of the dryer. Bring back the clothesline!

- Encourage everyone to hang or fold clothing that does not require washing. Many laundry loads grow huge because we are too lazy to put clothes away.

- Reading care labels saves a lot of grief.

- Ring around the collar? Shampoo dissolves body oils.

▓ Clothes fade less if washed inside out.

▓ Avoid 100 percent cotton shirts! They are a real headache to maintain, and they don't keep their fresh, pressed look.

▓ Keep stains off your clothes. Wear an apron. (Personally, I wish someone would invent an adult bib!)

▓ Get a good book on stain removal.

▓ Hang knits, like pants, over a hanger. They will keep better.

▓ Don't throw wet clothes in a heap—you will never get the wrinkles out. Or the mildew.

▓ Purchase a good lint roller or carding brush to keep your clothes neat.

▓ Always wash reds alone.

▓ Some dry-cleaners offer a bulk rate, such as ten pounds for $12. They pretreat and dry-clean, but you do the ironing.

▓ Avoid buying "dry-clean only" clothing.

▓ Wash woolens carefully if you don't dry-clean them. Once wool shrinks, it gets "felted" and cannot be stretched back.

▓ Rayon does not hold up well to home washing. As a rule, it must be dry-cleaned.

▓ Not all silks are alike. If you buy anything silk, check first to see if it can be washed.

▓ Take advantage of dry-cleaning seasonal specials:

   Spring: drapes, pillows, blankets, spreads

   Fall: hunting clothes, sleeping bags

   Prom time: formals

When you do not hang still-clean clothes after wearing, you waste...

- Natural resources due to the power used to run the washer and dryer.

- The clothes themselves, since constant washing and drying is hard on clothes.

- Much, *much* more of your own time, considering the lugging, sorting, washing, drying, folding, ironing, more lugging, and putting away—compared to hanging something in the closet. No brainer.

Shoe Care

- Shoe repair is often worth the price. Always check with a cobbler to see if your shoes can be repaired.

- Replace heels, not shoes. The rubber end of the heel is much less expensive to replace than the entire heel. (Sigh. Would that we could replace other kinds of "heels," huh?)

- After you wear shoes awhile, take them to a shoe-repair shop. The cobbler will study the soles to determine where to put nylon taps to save on wear.

- Most children's shoes are not repairable, nor are cheaper shoes or shoes that are plastic.

- Keep leather work boots greased. Waterproof winter boots.

- Scuff marks are tough to remove. Use cream polish on shoes before they get scuffed.

- Save old shoes for doing yard work. Have you ever mowed your lawn wearing new sneakers?

Home Care

When most women were at home all day, they could routinely clean, shake, and bake; each day had a special chore. Fast-forward to today's single-parent or nuclear family. Add commuting to a full-time job, ferrying the kids to an endless assortment of activities, trying to maintain sound nutrition, recharging your batteries somehow so you can stay awake past 8:00 P.M.—all while dust accumulates on the VCR, layers of exploded food build up in the microwave, and thick soap scum coats the shower. Whether you are at home during the day or chasing off to work, housekeeping is a big job. Here are some tips to keep the buffalo from roaming in your home:

- Don't buy fancy cleaners. Products with less advertising money are often just as good or better—people wouldn't buy them unless they perform. Vinegar and baking soda each have thousands of uses.

- As I suggested before, visit a janitorial supply shop. Many commercial products come in concentrated form, are much less expensive overall, and are significantly better in performance than most grocery store supplies. I have a gallon jug of window washing concentrate. It cost me about as much as two of those spritz bottles of blue stuff. I add one teaspoon of concentrate to several quarts of water. I have had this gallon jug for ten years and plan to bequeath it to my grandchildren.

- I took a long time to learn that more is not always better. For instance, if a little bit of a cleaning product did a good job, I thought a whole *cup* of it in my bucket would be better. Cleaning products come with dilution ratios for a reason: Too much of a good thing gunks up what you are cleaning.

- Do not spray windows with the garden hose unless you like to look through hard-water stains.

▪ Liquid bleach diluted in water in a spray bottle will disinfect nearly everything. But be careful! It will also bleach spots all over your clothing—or anything else "bleachable."

▪ Try using a couple of Gramp's denture cleaning tablets in a stained toilet. Flush first.

▪ Cheap detergents have an abundance of filler. The cheapest part of laundry detergent is salt, which softens water. This gives you less cleaning power.

▪ If your coffee table has dust on it, so do your sofa and chairs. (Same dust.) Vacuum your furniture or wipe it clean.

▪ Vacuum your mattress every couple of months. Invisible mites thrive on flakes of dead skin. Discard your filter bag immediately.

▪ Run your pillows and blankets through "air fluff" in your dryer. Better yet, air them out on the clothesline in the backyard.

▪ The best bet for hard floors of any kind is a commercial-quality dust mop and water-based dust spray.

▪ Use a pH-neutral product when damp mopping; the shine will last longer. Dirt is acidic, and an alkaline cleaner will loosen the wax finish.

▪ Never use an acrylic-based product on a no-wax floor.

▪ Wash and wax simultaneously? You know—those products you squirt on your floor that do it all? Let's think about this for a minute. Where do you think the dirt goes? Do you think that maybe, just maybe, it is picked up, distributed evenly, and firmly locked in place when the wax dries?

For easy oven-cleaning, warm your oven, turn it off, and place a small bowl of ammonia inside. Close the door and let it sit overnight. Wipe your oven clean in the morning. Soak your oven racks in a towel-lined tub with ammonia and hot water.

Do not keep aluminum foil under the oven elements. So the experts say.

Vacuum under your refrigerator regularly. This is where you find the fan and the condenser. You will also find pet hairs and dust balls.

Empty the clothes dryer lint trap. Why don't we do this? A full trap makes your dryer work harder and can be a fire hazard.

Clean out your toaster often. Feed the crumbs to the birds.

Make your microwave sparkle. Heat a cup of water for two or three minutes in the microwave. Let it sit awhile. Wipe the microwave clean inside. (Caution! Stay clear of your microwave when heating *anything*. Some have exploded.)

Do not put anything wooden in the dishwasher—especially your chopping block. Heat dries the wood *and* the glue that holds these things together.

Do not use a laminated wooden chopping block as a hot pad.

Never wash your china in an aluminum pan. You may end up with gray, pencil-thin lines that are impossible to get out. Do not use very hot water, either, which causes "crazing," which are small lines and cracks in glass.

Clean your hot water heater every year.

■ The hot water heater is your friend in the shower but not in the wallet. Turn it down to 120 degrees and save around 10 percent on your utility bill. And do *not* let hot water run down the drain needlessly!

■ Hold a flashlight to your furnace filter. If the light is partially blocked, replace the filter.

■ A computer should not be in a damp place, or a place that gets too hot or cold.

The Vacuum Cleaner

This appliance gets special attention because we treat it like...well, like dirt. We really need to clean up our act and pay more attention to this important piece of equipment. For instance, your vacuum may be a super-deluxe model, but it will work no better than its filtering system.

You may be convinced by slick sales gimmicks that you have to buy a $1000 vacuum if you really want to keep your carpets clean. In many cases you can do as good a job with a $200 model if you change your bags a *lot*. Think how many bags $800 could buy!

A vacuum cleaner will lose between 25 and 50 percent efficiency after only ½ cup of fine dust accumulates in the bag. If your bag is too full, your vacuum will grind heavy dirt into your floor. (Got you on this one, didn't I?) This dirt acts like tiny scissors and cuts the fiber of your carpet. Pet hair and dandruff rot in the bag in any humidity at all. Dust mites thrive in the dark, humid environment of your filter bag. When you turn on your machine, microscopic pores act like little doorways—baby dust mites *explode* into the room. Grossed out yet?

■ Use double-density, anti-bacterial vacuum cleaner bags. They are more expensive but better for your health.

■ Check the revolving brush roller on your vacuum cleaner. Long hair and string are death to a vacuum.

- Regularly change the belt on your vacuum cleaner motor. How regularly? You know the smell.

- When buying a vacuum, check with the folks who repair them to find your best buy. I bought an excellent commercial vacuum from the janitorial shop for one-third its retail price. It was an overhauled trade-in. It has outlived and outperformed any other vacuum I've owned. That thing and I are a team.

- Become attached to your vacuum attachments: clean blinds, edge along walls, reach difficult spots, clean furniture.

While We're on the Floor

- Vacuum often. Your carpet will last much longer. Manufacturers suggest vacuuming twice a week for normal traffic areas.

- Vacuum in two different directions—six times over a spot is recommended. No kidding. (Don't shoot the messenger.)

- Keep carpets warranty-worthy. Most factory warranties for carpets require proof that they have been professionally cleaned every 18 months.

- Be careful with rental machines when shampooing carpet. If you get the carpet too wet you might break down or dissolve the backing; too much detergent could leave a residue, which attracts more soil. Can't win, can we?

- Use carpet runners and entrance mats. I'm told this is a top tip.

I Don't Mean to Bug You

Standing by and letting perfectly awful bugs eat your perfectly wonderful home seems wasteful indeed. An exterminator friend offered some tips to keep bugs at bay:

- Do not keep firewood in or alongside your home. It is job security for my friend.

- Do not keep a dirty house; be careful with food, crumbs, garbage, and scraps. Call in the spaniel!

- Vacuum as often as you can, especially if you have a spaniel.

- Bark or wood chip ground cover around the house is not sensible. Decaying material is an attraction for insects.

- Keep the foundation area of your home clean.

- Insect problems *do not get better.* If they are caught early, a barrier service outside will cost much less.

- When people see ants, where do they put bait canisters? Inside the house. "Why would you want to attract bugs?" said my friend. This is good use for your cayenne pepper. Sprinkle a barrier. You'll have those pesky critters doing the Mexican Hat Dance. Maybe this is where we got the term *antsy*.

> *Smart Think:*
>
> The energy saved from recycling one aluminum can is enough to operate a TV for three hours.

- Use bug spray with extreme caution; read the label, and keep it far away from children. It's lethal stuff.

Precycling

Want to save money on your garbage bill? Start by auditing your shopping cart. For instance, consider something as harmless as an individual lunch-box-sized serving of chocolate cake:

■ You are paying much more for the individually wrapped serving.

■ You are spending your money on junk food that has no redeemable food quality.

■ You are creating potential litter. Do your taxes pay for street cleaning?

■ You are creating garbage to go to your local landfill. Do your taxes pay for landfill maintenance?

> **Recycle. Better yet...*precycle!***

Utilities

If we ever turned a light on our waste, we would start by shining it on our natural resources and utilities. Electricity, gas, the phone, water, garbage—we use utilities daily, and we pay for that use, whether to a municipality, a corporation, a co-op, or a well driller. Every turn of the faucet, flick of the switch, or toss of the trash costs money.

Electricity

Three kitchen appliances compete with each other for "most use of electricity in a single day." They are the stove, the refrigerator (especially auto-defrost types), and the chest freezer.

Three that share the title of "lowest use of electricity in a single day" are the clock, the garbage disposal, and the crockpot.

In your house, the heaters, air conditioner, and water heater are energy-consuming culprits, with your water bed and clothes dryer close behind. Three more of the lowest users of power are the vacuum cleaner, the sewing machine, and the VCR.

Gas

Depending on where you live, gas may be a sensible method to cut fuel or power cost. Gas appliances usually cost less to operate, but you can buy a whole lot of kilowatt-hours for the price of investing in gas appliances!

Call your electric company and ask the price of a thermal unit of power. Do the same with your gas company. Factor in the cost of the heating device or appliance. Compare. It's that simple.

Heating and cooling your home accounts for as much as 60 percent of your energy bill. Check the appendix for tips on cutting this cost without cutting comfort.

Insulate!

Insulation reduces drafts and keeps temperature constant. The most important areas to insulate are the attic, the floors, and the walls.

Windows

Up to 33 percent of a home's heat goes out the windows and doors. Taking energy-saving measures in the window department is well worth your time and money.

Storm windows and doors insulate by creating air space. Windows are rated by "U" value: The lower the rating, the better the efficiency but the higher the price. Glass storm windows (in metal, vinyl, or wooden frames) are the most effective and the most durable. You can devise your own storm windows from the following:

- Clear plastic, taped to the inside frame (neither durable nor appealing).

- Mylar (more durable, easier to see through).

- Rigid plastic, cut to fit the window.

Weather Stripping and Caulk

You can lose as much as 40 percent of your heat if your home is not weatherized. Air leaks are among the largest sources of energy loss. The most common need for weather stripping is under a door. A quarter-inch gap at the bottom of your door could waste as much warm air as a three-inch hole in the side of your house!

Check for air leaks by holding a damp hand near an area. Close all the doors and turn off the fans when searching and concentrate on these problem areas:

around chimneys	recessed lighting
fireplace damper	electric boxes
ceiling fans	around doors and windows
attic access	around plumbing

Your utility company might offer rebates for weather stripping and caulk. When combined with weather stripping, caulk could save enough energy in the first year to pay for itself. Caulk is normally applied where two different materials meet or where a space is evident.

Water, Water Nowhere, and Not Enough to Drink

We are running out of water. That is what some areas of our country are coming to because of drought. And maybe a little bit because of our misuse.

The National Rural Water Association says each person needs one hundred gallons of water every day. Do you pay for your water? If so, there are many ways to cut consumption *with no sacrifice in comfort to you.*

▪ If the tap is left running, the NRWA claims the average person uses up to ten gallons of water while brushing his or her teeth. Suppose you have a family of four and everyone brushes twice each day. That means 80 gallons down the drain each day. This sounds a bit far-fetched to me, but I didn't do the study.

■ If you are a man, do you leave the hot water running while shaving? Consider the cost of the power to keep the water hot, as well as the water you use—on average, 20 gallons of hot water down the drain.

■ Do you have a leaky faucet? Sixty drops per minute loses 113 gallons per month, or 1356 gallons each year.

■ Do you have a leaky toilet? A leaky toilet can break the budget! Check for leaks by adding blue food coloring to the tank, waiting ten minutes, then checking the water inside the bowl. If you see color, fix the leak at once!

Car Talk

Along with our home or our children's education, cars rank high in competition for our income. We invest an inordinate amount to own them. Caring for them as best we can is only logical. Yet most of us have barely enough money to make payments, let alone repair or maintain a car properly. What happens when our maintenance dollar shrinks or disappears? Expensive breakdowns.

Owning and Operating

Very few of us can manage without a car...but do we really know how much of our hard work goes to maintain that hunk of steel grinning out in the garage? If you factor operating costs which include gas, oil, maintenance, and tires with ownership costs which include taxes, depreciation, finance charges, registration, insurance, and license fees, you may be facing a significant daily cost. Stick the insurance spike from a teenage driver into that equation and, well, ouch.

Do the Repairs Yourself—Sometimes!

You can learn to do many things yourself, especially with older cars, but most repairs on modern cars should be left to trained technicians. Modern cars come with sophisticated computers and electronic systems. Mechanics tell me many a car owner has moved a wire or a hose to save on repair bills only to face big bills later.

You can do some things to save money as a car owner:

- Take a car-care course to learn simple procedures.

- Don't be fooled; most modern cars do not need tune-ups. In these days of new fuel-injection engines, a running problem is probably related to a car's computer or emissions system.

- Go to the busiest gas station in town for fuel. You will be less likely to get water in the gas, and you will often find the best prices, too.

- Find a garage with a reputation for integrity and good work.

- Pump your own (unless you live in New Jersey or Oregon).

- Whatever you do, change your oil. We change oil every 2500 miles and are convinced this is a key element in avoiding expensive repair.

- Super-fast lubes may be okay, but you can usually find better prices and more experienced mechanics at a full-service automobile-repair shop.

- Don't be an "easy sell." When the mechanic holds your dirty air filter under your nose and says, "This filter is filthy," say, "Why, thank you for alerting me. I will tend to the matter promptly." Then buy one at a discount store—they are simple to install!

- Ditto for the windshield washer fluid unless it's included with your service.

- Rotate your tires every five to ten thousand miles! This is a money-saving tire tip.

- If your car is out of alignment, you will go through new tires at an alarming rate.

- Brand-name tires are not always the best quality. Some other brands have better tires that cost less. Remember what the tire guy said: "Just because it's round and black doesn't mean it's the same."

- If tires are on sale, be sure mounting and balancing are included in the price. You should try to get an alignment included in the service, too. Ask for the "out-the-door" price *before* you purchase.

- Under-inflated tires cause greater wear and lower gas mileage. The inflation level is stamped into the side of each tire.

- One of the worst things you can do to a car is drive short distances without giving it a chance to get warm. In very short distances, your muffler does not get hot enough to burn off condensation. (For every four gallons of gas you burn, you reap about one gallon of condensation.) And what does water do to metal?

- Here is another reason to cruise once a week: If your car never warms enough to eliminate the products of combustion, the engine will sludge. This leads to excessive mechanical wear and tear. (Make sure you change your oil regularly!)

- Air-conditioners cut gas mileage by about 2.5 miles per gallon.

- If you replace your exhaust system, buy a lifetime system and keep your receipt. As long as you intend to keep your car, that is.

- If you hear a squeak, get the brakes checked. Repairs are more costly and driving is more dangerous if you wait.

■ Unless you are dealing with a trusted mechanic, be suspicious if anyone says you need shocks or struts. My sources say this is one of the biggest waste areas in automotive care. Do your own test: push a corner of your vehicle down. It should immediately return to its original position with no extra bounce. Test all four corners.

■ Most front-wheel or four-wheel-drive cars have CV boots. These are rubber "bellows" that protect the axle joints from dust and dirt. If the boot tears, the cost of replacing the axle is not far off. This must be fixed *at once,* and it is not cheap. How can you tell if you need boots? Besides seeing the tear, once the boot has a hole or rip, grease will sling all around the area. Take a flashlight and slide under the front to check where the axle connects with the wheel.

■ A paste of baking soda on battery terminals can remove corrosion.

(More on conservation and precycling in Appendix 3.)

> In Scripture mankind is viewed as a steward of God's riches, ordered in the creation narrative to "subdue the earth, to till and keep it." This provides us with a unique and privileged responsibility to share in God's work of creation. At the heart of stewardship is an understanding of the "symbiosis" of all things, in which the whole of creation works harmoniously together.
>
> —R. K. HARRISON

CHAPTER 9

Discover Your Creative Genius

In Other Words...

Look for the path of least expenditure. This principle is by far the most challenging, but when the challenge meets with success, this principle is by far the most fun.

How do you find the path of least expenditure? You learn a few simple skills that train you to use your brain and your mouth before you ever put your hands to a task. Before I plead my case for brainpower as your first defense against a limited budget, let's have a story!

The Adventures of Frugal Woman & Wonder Man

Years ago when we lived on the lake, we were at the end of our rope. We had absolutely no extra money due to high medical expenses, yet because of a change in the neighborhood, we needed to shore up a gaping rip in our land that was about three feet high and twenty feet long. What we needed was a retaining wall.

We priced lumber till we were blue in the face, and everything we looked into had about the same price tag: $1000. So Joe and I went outside and just sat down and stared at the area and kept thinking: *What can we do to create a retaining wall? How can we find the path of least expenditure?* Then it hit us: What do you have an abundance of when you live on a glaciated lake? Rock.

Joe rolled up his sleeves and went to work—it was backbreaking work—but in no time we had an awesome rock wall. Financial outlay: zero. Except for all that liniment.

~ ~ ~

Use Your Noggin and Just Say Aaaahhh (Open Your Mouth)

Our retaining wall story says it all. Finding the path of least expenditure causes you to use your noggin. It also compels you to color and to think outside the lines. In the above case, we got stuck on our first thought that our retaining wall must be made of wood. Staring our problem in the face, we began to shift our thinking from wood to concrete to cinder block to rock.

To use your creative genius, don't be afraid to break a few rules and do something different. For instance, if finances are a tad low and you are trying to use things up, would the world come to a rapid end if you had cereal for dinner? Of course it wouldn't. Oh, but your husband would complain, would he? So stick a meatball in his cornflakes.

When using your *noggin,* your goal is to determine if that expenditure you are facing can be accomplished:

1. at no financial cost

2. at a significantly reduced cost

3. at full cost with some slack

4. at full cost

When using your *mouth,* your goal is to ask a few questions. Each of the questions falls under the "ownership" principle we talked about in chapter 4. From dealing with a contractor to booking a trip, consider these questions:

1. Is this your lowest price?

2. Do you expect a sale on this item soon?

3. What is the most prudent way for me to financially accomplish my goal?

4. Do you have any suggestions as to how I can do this task without spending much money (or any money)?

5. Also ask yourself this question: *What am I not willing to sacrifice for the sake of least expenditure?*

No Cost

The retaining wall is an example of finding a solution that required no financial outlay. We already had a sturdy wheelbarrow, an endless supply of rock, and several pair of sturdy work gloves. Getting the rock from the beach to the worksite was labor intensive. Stacking the rock took some skill, which Joseph developed as he progressed. (He did consult one of our how-to books.) The job was accomplished on a weekend, so we lost no time from weekday work...and I was joking about the liniment.

Smart Think:

Am I so afraid of rejection that I won't even ask a polite question?

Would Joseph have preferred to spend his weekend relaxing? Sure, but he had the right attitude, rolled up his sleeves, used what he had, and creatively went to work.

Whenever Joe and I are facing an undertaking, we immediately go into "noggin mode." Can we use nails, screws, hardware, lumber, paint, or fixtures that we have on hand? Can we find a way to meet our goal for free? Can we think of a satisfactory alternative to spending money?

As an example, we often fill our vases with ferns, branches, flowers, and pine boughs that we gather from outside instead of purchasing flowers.

Reduced Cost

If some expenditure is required, can the chore at hand be accomplished with minimal expense? Can you invest sweat equity into a project that legally or realistically requires a professional? Are you a savvy enough consumer to seek bids, learn prices, and cut a good deal without sacrificing quality? Call the experts and ask questions. If your project centers around home improvement, visit one of the bigger stores that cater to weekend fixer-uppers and are staffed with pros who gladly give advice and instruction. I have benefited from their expertise countless times...without blinking my baby gray green eyes.

Creative genius applies to every single aspect of our lives, not just big improvement projects.

We had an old cocker called Teddy. Teddy lost her teeth, her hearing, her eyesight, and slept under my side of the bed where she snored like an old man. She needed special care—and special food. The hard crunchy kibble just wouldn't work any longer. The special foods sold for toothless dogs were a bit spendy. We bought kibble created for older dogs but added water to soften it before we fed the old girl every day. We found the path of least expenditure.

Another example: We fly into Dulles International Airport quite often. The cost of a cab into Washington, D.C., is almost $50. How could we get from Dulles to Washington by using the path of least expenditure? We thought about this, and then we asked: How do people who work at Dulles commute each day?

Lo and behold, we were perfectly welcomed to take an employee shuttle...for $2.50 each.

One more: We have a majestic grove of trees on our front lawn. Tall, mature birch trees are laced with Douglas fir. Our granddaughter finds the grove under the trees magical. I intend to make a cement "mushroom" table for Ellen so she and I can sit under the cool branch canopy during the heat of summer and sip make-believe tea. I am already thinking about my path of least expenditure. I know for sure that I will use some old pails for my mold. My creativity has kicked in and I plan to use an old trash pail lid for my mushroom top. Why, as I sit here and think about it, I may even press some colored tile pieces onto our mushroom tea table. I could even write her name! Gosh, I could make grooves for marbles, indentations for our teacups...

The Adventures of Frugal Woman & Wonder Man

We once chose to replace our kitchen floor. I'd grown weary of the patchwork rug I'd made from carpet samples, cute as it was. We knew we had to lay plywood on the subflooring that lay beneath the carpet. The cost of covering the plywood was simply not in our budget. Just as we once sat and stared at a gaping rip in our land, we sat on the kitchen floor and thought some more.

Okay. We have to invest in plywood to cover the subfloor, but what can we do to the surface? Bingo! Wonder Man to the rescue: "We'll create a faux tongue-and-groove look."

Off we drove to buy plywood, a metal yardstick for use as a straight edge, some persimmon-colored floor paint, and spar varnish. Joseph used a utility knife to score lines into the plywood, creating a "wood floor" design. We painted the plywood and varnished it with a protective coating, and the kitchen took a brand-new look. A pretty spectacular brand-new look, I might add.

Expenditures need not be huge nor involve your home. Here's another example of finding the path of least expenditure:

I do not like to bring a big bouquet of flowers when I visit someone in the hospital. It is too much hassle for the medical staff to maneuver in a cluttered room and too much hassle for the poor caregiver who has to haul all of that stuff home along with the patient. Yet I do like to bring something.

When I visit someone in the hospital, I swing by the dollar store and buy a pretty vase. I then visit a large supermarket to purchase a single carnation with some greens. I often bring a bit of raffia or ribbon from home to tie round the vase. My gift is simple, thoughtful, and sensible (carnations last a very long time).

Had I purchased the same thing at the hospital store, the price would be *at least* three times more expensive than the $2.50 this usually costs me. Am I being "cheap" because I looked for the path of least expenditure? No, I'm being smart.

~ ~ ~

Full Cost with Some Slack

Suppose you must buy carpet. You've researched types of carpet and know that nylon is the most resilient, olefin is the most naturally stain resistant, polyester has the most vivid colors, and natural fibers are the most difficult to clean. You've considered fiber, durability, weight, and twist rate. You've considered quality and price. And you have found a reputable dealer—a dealer who won't budge from his price. You want to deal with his firm, and the cost is actually within reason and within budget. It's time to dicker. Ask if he will throw in the carpet pad or at least reduce the price of the pad. (Heads up! Experts tell me high quality carpet pad is critically important when buying carpet.) You might ask if installation can come for free, especially if you promise to have the room spic and span and completely empty with the old carpet removed. Or ask if the firm will include removing and hauling away the old carpet within the bid price.

Afraid to dicker? I've read that Americans are part of a small minority of people in the world who do not haggle over price. I am not advocating that you cheat someone out of fair profit— you must never do that—but do not be afraid to ask if there is room to dicker. Politely.

When we moved into our present house, we budgeted a certain amount for a sofa and love seat. We found the ones we wanted, but they were $400 over our budget. I really wanted that couch—you know, the one that slides halfway to Jersey when leaned against. So what did I do? For one thing, I made certain I was dealing with the manager. I told him honestly how much over budget the couch and loveseat were. He knocked $300 off the already low sale price. Just like that. Now I ask you: What if I hadn't opened my mouth? Would I have paid the extra $400?

You Want Proof? I'll Give You Proof!

Here is a valuable tip, almost always guaranteed to result in lower cost. Next time you book a motel room and are given a price, ask: "Is that your lowest price?"

When booking a motel room (or checking in), you will often be quoted a rack price. Unless you already are a preferred customer or the season is at its peak, this question is almost guaranteed to be answered, "No, that is not our lowest rate." You should not only ask for their lowest price but also ask if they have additional discounts available for AARP members, warehouse store memberships, professional rates, and auto club rates.

When I prepared to travel to Boise, Idaho, I called an 800 operator and got a number for the Boise Tourist Information Center. I had a nice chat with the person at the Information Center and explained we would be there for a week and needed inexpensive lodging. The Center sent me a magazine all about the town that included several choices for various places to stay. I drew up my requirements on our letterhead and faxed my request for rates to seven moderately priced places. Of the three that responded, one put us in a great area, included cooking facilities, and only cost around $30 each night. Because we had the magazine, we could study the town in advance so we didn't feel like complete strangers when we arrived, and we were able to get in on some of the activities. Notice that we didn't automatically call what we perceived to be a budget motel and simply book our room.

I often shake my head and think to myself, *What if I had not asked?*

When we moved to our new house, we needed a fence. We were perfectly willing to install this fence ourselves, but when we figured the cost of corner posts and wooden posts at eight-foot spacing, we faced a pretty spendy proposition. I called a fencing contractor and asked a simple question: "Excuse me, kind sir," I said, "is it possible that you have a pile of posts that are hanging around in your yard that are all weathered and ugly but still in good condition that you would really, *really* like to get rid of because your wife is hounding you to clean up the yard?" "Why yes, I do," he responded. The posts were one-fifth the cost, and we had a nice "older" look that we prefer anyway.

Talk about asking! I must share another escapade because of the remarkable results that came from my ownership principle and asking a few polite questions.

The Adventures of
Frugal Mother-of-the-Groom

Joshua got married. The wedding was in New Orleans—a world, we were told, unto itself, loaded with stately charm. As parents of the groom, the rehearsal dinner was our responsibility. We wanted it to reflect the joy of the occasion, as well as the majestic splendor of the area. And though we were fully prepared to cover any expenses associated with the dinner, the principles outlined in this book kicked in. (Principles probably imprinted on every molecule in my body.)

Please understand, the issue of the rehearsal dinner was not about skimping. Regardless of the circumstance, I *automatically* began to think and to ask. This time, the result was a night to remember.

Instead of its normal banquet hall, a world-famous restaurant provided a majestic suite of rooms for the same price. Why? Ownership. I'd conversed with the manager often and developed rapport. She knew I wasn't trying to "skin" her. We paid the full price for a full-course meal for 30 guests. Extra amenities were complimentary because I arrived the day of the dinner and helped her staff set tables.

Flowers for the dinner were critical. I met with a florist and gave him ownership. "Don't spare a thing," I told him. "We want flowers everywhere. But we don't want a bunch of dopey, predictable sprays down the middle of the tables, all dots and dashes and no pizzazz."

I told him we wanted guests to see each other, to feel gaiety in a sophisticated setting. He came through.

The head table nearly collapsed under the huge arrangement of massive flowers of every color and size imaginable. This was the florist's tribute to the bride and groom. The long guest tables were bedecked with nonstop ferns and ivy, a serpentine trail down their centers accentuated with lilies as big as pie plates and roses of every color, carnations, daisies, and more. Our florist bill was less than $300, and that included the bride's bouquet. Why? The rehearsal dinner was on a Friday night. Florists often empty their coolers on Friday night, much of their excess stock going to dumpsters. Our spectacular explosion of flowers was from a florist who participated in our fantasy for the evening, was fair, and who did not waste.

Place cards were a simple matter of gold ink on pale pink card stock. A memento for each guest of a small jar of Montana jam, draped with colorful Mardi Gras beads, was symbolic of bringing two families together. But something was missing.

Candles! What to do about candles? Candle rental was absurdly expensive. Time to think creatively. We visited the local Hallmark for candles, used small crystal votive holders from the restaurant's supply room (offered for free if I arrived early to wash them), placed candles among the flowers, dimmed the lights, and the evening was spellbinding. To top it off, two young nieces, cute as buttons, brought their violins to serenade "Cousin" and his new bride.

We were not responsible for the professional photographer. He was found, by the way, through a phone call to the photography department of a local college. Budding (amateur) photographers are sometimes quite skilled and charge less for their services.

～　～　～

Full Cost

You are not pond scum if you pay full retail price. Not all of life is a bargain. Some things are neither free nor even inexpensive. In some cases, the "path of least expenditure" may very well *be* the price that is asked.

Frugal means smart. Frugal does not mean fanatic or stupid. I don't think I would try to haggle, for instance, if a surgeon was standing over my body in a dire situation. "Pardon me, is that your lowest price?" just before his first cut would be a tad wacko.

There are certain local merchants whom I support with my business. I deliberately shop in their stores because I recognize that they *need* my business. I would never once consider haggling over price in these places. One such place is our local Christian bookstore. I recognize the ministry this store serves in our community. I feel it my obligation—and honor—to patronize that store. So would you.

Using Your Noggin

Catalogs and magazines are invaluable tools when developing your creative genius. I pore over catalogs as if I were studying for midterms at Harvard. By studying catalogs I am able to hone my skills with prices, find amazing decorating and style ideas, and put my noggin to work. *Hmmm...can I do that?* Yesterday I saw a huge door wreath in a catalog that appealed to me. The wreath seemed to be nothing but a mass of tiny, white twinkle lights. It cost $75 plus shipping and handling.

Pshaw, I thought. I can do that. I will buy the largest grapevine wreath I can find at the discount store and wrap several strings of lights around the wreath with lights I buy at the warehouse store. I expect to have that fabulous wreath on our door to greet guests this holiday season for around $10. *That* is the path of least expenditure.

I occasionally purchase through catalogs, but when I do, I factor in shipping, possibility of return, and the possibility of being hoodwinked. Catalogs can be a boon to the busy person, can limit expenditure since you are not in a shopping environment designed to make you spend, can give you an awesome selection, and can sometimes lead you to a unique find.

Remember the fabulous sale I stumbled upon at a distant outlet? When Joseph and I were in that town recently, I made a dash for the store, armed with a copy of their latest catalog, which I had dog-eared. A white blouse in the catalog caught my eye, but $42? Not in this lifetime! Straight past the retail store I marched, catalog in hand, and into their outlet I went. I began the search, and then I found it: perfect in every way, but wrinkled. $9.98. Sold.

Creative Gifting

A good place to start developing your creative genius is in gift giving, especially if you have a limited income.

One of the most popular ways to honor another is to present that person a gift. History would be incomplete without mention of gift exchanges between countries, rulers, and ethnic groups—even between wise men and a baby! We bring flowers, bake bread, buy toys and trinkets, and elaborately wrap our presents, all to show others how much they mean to us. Presenting the perfect gift brings us a moment of supreme joy. Gift giving is one area where I shine!

Gift giving is not only a very expensive assault on our checkbook but also a real challenge when trying to find the right gift for the right person—at the right cost. I use ten strategies for gift giving, strategies that I have shared on television, on radio, in books, magazines, and now with you.

1. It *is* the thought that counts. Cost is not the main factor in the gifts we give. Intent, effort, and meaning come through loud and clear when we give a gift. A gift should honor a person, regardless of cost.

2. Color outside the lines. Don't be predictable, especially when you are looking for a way to present your gift. Just about anything can be used to hold your gift:

flower pots, enamel pans, bowls, bags, pillow cases...and the ubiquitous basket. Why not give a gift of one-dozen cookies standing upright in a long, skinny basket? Attach a card that pledges "The Twelve Months of Cookies."

The Adventures of Wonder Man

This is how Wonder Man got his name:

When I turned 50, Joseph began "gifting" me 25 days before my birthday and continued for 25 days after. He called it "The Fifty Days of Birthday" and brought me a present every day. Some days it was nothing more than a favorite candy bar. On the day of my birthday it was a big crockery bowl, so someday I could "make cookies with the grandkids." He wanted our future grandchildren to have memories of Gram and that bowl. What a guy! One day he walked in with a shirt pocket filled with tiny shooting stars. "I picked these for you," he said. And I said "You are a wonder." He is, you know. And I am blessed.

3. Plan ahead. This gets your brain in gear and gives you a chance to buy in advance. Does anyone in your family like to play golf? Buy golf gizmos and gadgets at the end of golf season and save them for birthdays or for Christmas. (Maybe this was a bad example...er, does golf season ever end?)

4. Presentation is everything. (This is the next principle you will learn.) If you can't fold straight corners on gift wrap, use gift bags. Everything you hand to another

person, whether a dollar bill when buying something, your hand in a handshake, or a gift, is an extension of you. You show your respect for the other person when you take care in presentation. A huge part of the thrill of the gift is in the wrapping. Has anyone ever handed you something in a store bag, unwrapped? Be honest— it didn't feel so special, did it?

5. When in doubt, give food. Enjoy the pure pleasure of filling a crinkle bag (a sandwich bag will do) with colorful penny candy and giving it to a child. Attach a small toy or bell (Caution! Consider the child's age and the possibility of choking!) and close it with curly ribbon. Magic.

   I like to fill empty toilet paper rolls with candy when a child is coming to dinner. I wrap the roll, tie curly ribbon on both ends, write the child's name with a Magic Marker, and put it on the child's plate.

   Toilet paper rolls wrapped in aluminum foil and crimped at their ends with colorful "star wire" make stunning place settings for New Year's Eve festivities. I put nuts inside.

6. When really in doubt, say something nice. When Mom turned 80, I called family members. "Tell me what you love most about Mom/Gram," I asked. We presented her with a framed declaration of "The 25 Things We Love About You," not the least of which was her amazing chocolate-chip cookies. Now I ask you: Does she treasure that gift?

   A friend of mine also turned 80. I called several of her closest friends and asked them to join us for high tea at a local restaurant. I told each friend to bring a synthetic flower and to prepare to tell us all why Gracie was just like that particular flower. I provided a vase for Grace to haul her flowers home. We ended up creating a touching tribute, a colorful bouquet, and a remarkable afternoon.

7. Study magazines and catalogs for gift ideas.

8. Make your own greeting cards. Use card stock, cut straight lines, and design your own card. If you don't like the homemade look, invest in plain white note cards and adorn them with elegant writing or stickers.

9. Always keep your eyes open for a gift idea. Walking on our beach one day, I found a long, smooth stone with a natural indentation. Lo and behold, I then found a smooth rock that fit into that indentation hand in glove. I gave it to a friend as a "mortar and pestle." It's become one of her treasures.

10. Keep a gift stash. Think about friends and family when you stumble onto blowout sales. Buy Christmas ornaments and seasonal gifts *the day after* the holiday, and stash.

By the way, gift certificates may not seem very Christmassy, but the money goes twice as far the week after Christmas. Speaking of Christmas...

The Holidays

Earlier in the book I invited you to ask yourself a simple question: What will I waste during this holiday season?

Year after year our entire family vowed to keep Christmas simple, to keep it holy, to keep the gifts to a minimum. Yet we didn't, and I was the greatest offender. (One can get carried away with blowout sales and gift stashes and the joy of giving.) I put my foot down.

Smart Think:

I pledge to keep the next holiday season holy, simple, and peaceful.

We no longer give gifts at Christmas. Oh, sure, there is something minimal for the grandkids (a theme ornament), and I will always give Mom a box of chocolate-covered cherries, but the glut has stopped. We put emphasis, instead, on birthday presents.

This may seem strict and a little over the edge. Joseph has campaigned to at least hang stockings, and he is probably right. It is Christmas, after all. I just grew weary of the ho-ho-ho-oh-no, that's all. Just to prove I'm not a grump when it comes to holidays, I'll share some frugal tips to love the one you love.

Valentine's Day Genius

(Men: Simply change the pronoun to "she" or "her.")

1. Remember how you used to have regular eye contact and smile at each other? Do it again.

2. The next time he aggravates the tar out of you, laugh if off and don't take it so seriously.

3. Stand by the window, watch for him to come home, and then meet him at the door. This is way better than sticking your hand in the air to tell him to hush until you read the last paragraph or watch the last episode of your favorite show.

4. Soak his feet. Then give him a foot massage with warm oil. Use Canola if you have to—it doesn't matter. A foot massage is close to the top of the list of stress relievers and is definitely an act of selfless love.

5. Do you know what tops the list? A head massage. Run a soft brush through his hair and massage his temples. Have you ever gotten your hair done? You know how comforting it is to have your head rubbed.

6. Affirm him in front of others—and mean it.

7. Write a prayer just for him. Talk with your holy God. Thank Him for your mate. Pray for his protection, his health, and his well-being. Show your man the prayer and pledge to pray it every morning before you even open your eyes.

8. Write a love poem. It doesn't have to rhyme, it can be silly, and it can be mushy. Attach it to a balloon and tie it to his car antenna.

9. Sit him down and tell him *why* you love him. (This is especially important for men to do for their wives.) For instance, if I sit Joe down, I will tell him that two things I most admire in him are his utter lack of deception and his integrity (not to mention his servant's heart).

10. Be as Christ to each other.

A Few Creative Gift Ideas

- Use scraps of lumber to make a birdhouse or bird feeder.

- Use scraps of lumber to design signs of whimsy for a country kitchen or for someone's garden: Apples 4 Sale; Welcome; Herbs 10 Cents; Sit Long, Talk Much.

- Do you not have any scraps of lumber? Visit a building site.

- Find several chunky pieces of driftwood. Drill a hole through the center of each piece. Run strong wire through all holes until you have created a long (and heavy, trust me!) mobile. This adds a rustic touch to the outside of some homes.

- Do what we did with a dessert cookbook. One day we took it off the shelf and wrote this on the inside cover (you have my permission to do the same):

Dear Friend:

Cookbooks, like friendships, sometimes sit on shelves and don't get used. Let's do something about that! Would you kindly look through this book and choose a recipe that appeals to you? Return the book, make note of the recipe, and we will prepare it for you.

Joe & Cynthia

▪ Make a gift sack. The two key elements of *romantic* giving are spontaneity and surprise. Let me tell you about our gift sack. It is one of those white paper sacks with a paper handle from the produce department at the market. We wrote the words "Isle of View" (I love you) on the sack with blue Magic Marker. The current holder of the sack is responsible for the next "sack attack." I have it now. One day, when Joe is least expecting, he will walk to his car, or pull back the bed covers, or reach for his shoes—and he will find the sack. It might have a love note inside. Or a favorite candy bar. Or a meaningful gift. You get the idea.

▪ Make a special bridal gift. With a little bit of creativity, you can put together a spice and herb set that will be very much appreciated. Find interesting little bottles or jars, create your own labels, and buy the herbs at the local health food store for peanuts.

▪ Go to a kitchen gadget store and buy a pepper mill. *Shop!* Not all kitchen gadget stores are created equal! Some are very high-end in price. Look for good quality in a pepper mill. Buy some bulk peppercorns and assemble the box. Throw in a few bay leaves for good luck.

■ Present a child with an adventure gift certificate: take the child to the bakery, the meat market, a restaurant, a TV or radio station, a fire or police station, the animal shelter, and explore *behind the scenes*. Tour a local business! Call first.

I Knew You Was a-Comin' so I Baked a Cake!

I have a lot of fun with this demonstration at seminars. We're going to decorate a cake (or a muffin or a donut) together.

To me, few things are worse than someone's birthday going by without a birthday cake. Think of it—a birthday is the most special day of the year for a person. It is their very own day. Honor it! Bake a cake! Or buy a sponge cake at the bread outlet and have at it. Some ideas:

■ Put a handful of real chocolate chips into a strong, zip-lock baggie. Soak the baggie with the chips in very hot water till chocolate is melted. (When chocolate melts it retains its shape, so you have to mush it a bit.) Cut the *tiniest* tip off the corner of the baggie. (This does take some experimenting.) Now the fun! Gather the baggie in one hand and drizzle chocolate all over the cake. Color outside the lines! Let it drizzle on the plate! Just zigzag all over the place.

■ Here is a great addition to the chocolate drizzle, or a pretty touch on its own: Get a fine strainer and hold it over the cake. Gently shake about one teaspoon of powdered sugar into the strainer, moving it and shaking it all over the cake like fine dust.

■ Frost the cake. Put cake in the freezer first so you have a hard surface to frost. And dip your frosting knife in hot water from time to time. Once the cake is frosted, scatter colored sprinkles, curly ribbon, candies, and colored candles on top.

■ After the cake is frosted, wrap a ribbon around the base like a hat band. Then cover the top with coconut or with fresh edible flowers.

■ Use your creative genius. Does your friend like to crochet? Stick a couple of colorful crochet needles into the cake. Does your friend like to golf? Stick colorful golf tees all over the place. (Watch out, though. You don't want to put anything toxic in the cake!)

Creative Kid Stuff

■ Are your children coming home for the holidays, or do you have grandchildren visiting? Are they bored? Make a miniature golf course in your living room. Use oatmeal boxes, cups, boards, and books. Get creative! Use an upside-down umbrella as a golf club.

■ This is for the birds! Gather pine cones with the children. Roll the cones in peanut butter and then in bird seed. String outside on trees.

■ Gather some outdated dress-up clothes from your closet or storage. Put together fun ensembles for the kids.

■ Help your child to wrap a box for someone special. Fill it with hugs and kisses.

Creative Genius Around the House

The Top Five Home Improvements for Resale Value

1. Do a minor kitchen remodel. Kitchen remodels top the list of the most cost-efficient home renovations. According to the experts, you will recoup nearly 100 percent of the remodel costs when you sell.

2. Add a potty. Throw in an extra bathtub, and you've got a great return for your dollar if you sell. Also, the family will love you for it.

3. Do a major kitchen remodel. This is when you turn your place into a high-tech "smart home."

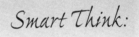

Smart Think:

Do your children or grandchildren want to spend their time playing with you, or with toys?

4. Turn your bedroom into a master suite. People want a refuge from the world and like to rest in the lap of luxury when they head for their bedrooms—sort of a private retreat. This can be accomplished with some clever furniture rearranging and decorating.

5. Stick in another bedroom. Insofar as resale is concerned, by the way, the attic seems to be preferred over the basement. Rooms that can be converted to family rooms, sewing rooms, craft rooms, and offices, are a big selling point.

Color Your World

How do you spruce up home sweet home on a shoestring? Easy. Just add color.

■ Choose one of the least-used colors in the room to accentuate with accessories.

■ Re-cover a couple of throw pillows with splashy prints.

■ Get a new lampshade.

■ Drape a colorful afghan on a sofa.

■ Pick wildflowers and stuff them in pitchers, jars, and baskets (find a way to keep a water supply in baskets).

■ You can spruce up a small space with crisp white accents.

■ Paint a piece of furniture.

Creative Window Ideas

■ Do you need storm windows? Call a carpenter who specializes in remodeling. Ask if he knows of any windows destined for the dump.

■ Make a small window appear larger by surrounding it with a stenciled border.

■ Widen a window by extending the track beyond its frame.

■ Is your window too tall? Use a valance or café curtains.

■ Paint designs on shades in children's rooms using bright colors. Paint the window trim to match one of the shade colors. (Shades are safer than blinds that come with long cords.)

Creative Projects

In case your home-improvement gene went south, here are a few time-tested projects that will inspire creativity around the house.

The Kitchen

Project: Re-cover kitchen chairs with calico, or use lightweight dishtowels. Any chair that has a removable seat can be covered in a flash. Look for fabric sales or remnants at the sewing center. Change the entire look of your kitchen by changing the seats and making a matching tablecloth. The same fabric can be used to line shelves, decorate canning jars, or to make a curtain. As a bonus,

1. With very little investment you've managed to perk up the kitchen.

2. The fabric can be changed as often as you like.

3. Friends will visit and say *"You* did that?!"

Project: Purchase dishtowels on sale, cut them in half, and hem the ragged side. You will end up with awesome cloth napkins without getting "soaked."

Project: Paint the legs of your kitchen table forest green and leave the top natural. As a bonus,

1. You may update a "dated" look.

2. You will add some "pop" to the room.

Project: Change the hardware on your cabinets. This can be spendy! Do you have furniture in the basement, garage, or shed from which you can "harvest" new hardware? Can you paint the existing hardware? Can you buy inexpensive wooden knobs and paint them a flashy color? Different hardware can upgrade a kitchen instantly.

The Bathroom

Project: Create more storage with baskets. Group similar items in each basket. Use hanging baskets to collect toiletries, hair-care products, pretty sponges, or a collection of soaps. As a bonus,

1. You have created more storage.

2. If you are using hanging baskets, you have created storage out of thin air.

3. You have added a new dimension to the bathroom with the hanging baskets.

Project: Make a patchwork rug for your bathroom using coordinated sample squares. As a bonus,

1. You've changed the look for minimal cost.

2. You won't slip when you step out of the tub.

3. The floor will be warm in winter.

The Dining Room

Project: Scatter straw flowers, colored leaves, and small gourds all over your table when entertaining in the fall. Do the same with small pine boughs or holly in the winter and flowers in the spring.

We have clear glass plates (from the dollar store) which we put on top of fresh-picked ferns or flowers we use as place settings. Stunning. As a bonus,

1. Rave reviews!

2. Dining will be fun.

The Living Room

Project: Frame a high-quality greeting card, calendar page, or magazine picture. I did. It's a picture of an old building in Provence, taken from a calendar, and it is ensconced in an old wooden frame that once held a certificate of merit. As a bonus,

1. Art on a shoestring.

2. This art can be changed as often as one likes.

Project: Change some lampshades, or paint some existing lampshades. One of those foam brushes works best. As a bonus,

1. You may see your living room in a whole new light.

2. You will remember to dust the top of your light bulbs.

The Children's Room

Project: Create a desk for your child by cutting down an old appliance box. Let the child decorate it with markers, stickers, or paint. Make a fort by draping a sheet over a card table. As a bonus,

1. Your child is given creative expression.

2. You didn't buy fancy play equipment.

The Bedroom

Project: Make your own nightstand. Put a round piece of wood on top of any kind of base (we have used open-faced cardboard filing cabinets). Cover it with a small tablecloth. For added drama, cover the top of the tablecloth with a shawl. As a bonus,

1. You have more storage space.

2. You have a great place to hide a cat bed.

3. You have a great place to hide a lot of things!

4. You found a great place to finally use that shawl in the drawer.

Creative Genius with Food

- Shred freshly peeled potatoes and toss in a bit of olive oil. Pack them into a waffle iron coated with nonstick spray. Ta-Da! Hash brown waffles!

- S-T-R-E-T-C-H your food. This is amazing but true: If you cut something into pieces, you have more and it goes further. We had a friend who cut steaks into pieces before he grilled them for a picnic. He always bought *less* meat than he needed, and he always had some left over. Rather than offering a selection of grilled steaks, he presented a selection of precut portions of different sizes. This always works—trust me. Try it yourself with three potatoes.

  - Bake one (stab it with a fork a few times and put it in microwave for 6 to 8 minutes).

  - Cut one in quarters and steam it (you can do this in the microwave, too).

- Slice one into thin slices and pan fry or steam them. Or cut the third one into small cubes, steam them, and top them with butter.

   Which potato served more people?

■   So many suggestions overlap! This could be in the "Use Things Up" chapter or the "Waste Not" chapter, but here it is: Make stir-fry. Stir-fry calls for creativity. Just assemble all your produce that is getting "long in the tooth" and fry it quickly. Use soy sauce if you like. Add thin strips of meat if you like. If you are ambitious, start one-half hour before cooking and marinate the meat pieces in a combination of 2 tablespoons soy sauce, 1 teaspoon cornstarch, and 2 tablespoons water. Cook some rice to stretch your stir-fry.

■   This is not exactly food, but it is one of those tips that I feel is valuable enough to pass on to you even though I tend to avoid the notion that to be frugal you have to save every piece of string and every pull tab from every milk carton you've ever purchased...

Ten Things to Do with That Empty Half-Gallon Plastic Milk Jug That You Shouldn't Have in the First Place Because Light Degrades the Nutrition of Milk Stored in Plastic

1. Use it as a juice jug. You will need a good funnel (you should have a good funnel on hand). Let the frozen juice concentrate defrost so you can pour it in the jug. Use a permanent marker to designate type of juice in the jug.

2. Use it as a water jug.

3. Use it to carry the dog's water when you're traveling and Fido comes along. Keep a sturdy bowl handy. Dogs get very thirsty in the car.

4. Dry it thoroughly and use it to store small, pourable grains, rice, or beans.

5. Do you have a bunch of kids? Use that same permanent marker to write a child's name on the jug. Each child has an individual jug. This is a good way for you to measure how much water the kids are drinking.

6. Fill it three-quarters full and freeze it. Use it in coolers.

7. Use it to make and store plant fertilizer. Mix a batch and keep it handy. Mark the container!

8. Put some beans or pebbles inside, screw the top back on, and use it as a children's toss game. (Careful! Too many beans or pebbles will turn it into a children's "bonk" game.)

9. Cut out part of one side and cut enough out of the handle to make a "hook." Put birdfeed inside and hang it on a sturdy branch. Punch a few small drainage holes in the bottom.

10. Ditto. But store clothespins inside. Consider where you hang this thing, though—presentation is everything! (As you will learn in the next chapter.)

The Adventures of Frugal Woman

I decided I had to work on muscle mass. (My friends who read this will double over with uncontrolled mirth.) Anyway, I planned to get myself a couple of those barbells that people use to do "reps." I asked my sister if she had an extra pair that she might not be using. (My sister could probably bench-press a '57 Pontiac.) She walked over to her fridge and pulled out a milk container with a handle. "Sand works best," she said. "Oh, dur," I said. I now have two half-gallon dumbbells partially filled with sand to match the gallon-capacity one sitting on my shoulders.

~ ~ ~

Creative Genius with Car Parts

Many of us are trying to keep that hunk of steel out in the garage on its tires. But parts on an older car are going to wear out. Enter firms that manufacture rebuilt car parts.

Did you ever think to ask your mechanic if he would use a remanufactured car part? Sources say that they are often just as good (and sometimes better) than new. We saved a couple of hundred dollars last year doing just this thing. Many remanu-factured car parts come with a warranty. It's worth a try.

CHAPTER 10

Presentation Is Everything... or Is It?

Walk This Way

$\mathcal{I}$'ve had nothing but fun with the presentation principle, and after promoting its merit to a crowd, I often challenge volunteers to compete in a "walk-a-thon." Whichever person in the group walks with the most confidence, the most élan, the most panache, gets a prize. In my book, that person already is a winner.

Presentation is about having confidence in yourself and in your appearance. It is about using pretty things. It is about joy in your surroundings. And it is about consideration toward others.

We may have iced and decorated a few cakes in the last chapter, but *presentation* is the maraschino cherry we put on the icing on the cake!

Is Presentation Everything?

I used to ask every audience to repeat after me: Presentation is everything! I wore that sentiment on my sleeve. I promoted the concept. I lived the principle to the max. Yet over time I began to wonder...*Is presentation everything?* Not if it's only surface play, or as Joseph would say, "all hat and no cattle."

If someone's intent is to act better, to look better, or to live better than others—and to flaunt that haughty attitude in behavior or thought, then, no, presentation is not everything.

We are told in Scripture to count others as better than ourselves. We are told the second greatest commandment is to love our neighbors. We are told to be like Christ. Our hearts and motives must always be guided by God the Holy Spirit and must always reflect the fruit of that guidance: love, joy, peace, patience, kindness, goodness, faithfulness, meekness, and self-control. Remember the two economies of life we talked about in chapter 1? In God's economy, these traits are not only manifest when we walk with Him, they are *expected*.

The Adventures of Frugal Woman

We had a big deck when we lived on the lake. One sunny, bluebird day, a friend reclined on the deck, took a swig of lemonade, and commented: "I wonder what the poor people are doing now?"

"Presentation" certainly was everything at that moment: a splendid afternoon, the lake as still as glass, our lake view gloriously framed by big Ponderosa pine trees, fresh-squeezed lemonade, well-fed dogs resting in the afternoon sun, food aplenty in the kitchen. How I wish I had the presence of mind to answer that insensitive question!

While I am certain that man spoke without thinking, the sentiment he revealed cut me to the bone. What *were* the poor doing at that moment? They were trying. Some were suffering and struggling to survive. Others were starving and dying.

Full Circle

So is presentation everything? We need to flip back to the attitude chapter for an answer to this question.

If we are not arrogant, if we are always aware of the plight of others, if we are good stewards, if we use our gifts and material belongings to the glory of God, the answer is yes. Presentation is "everything," in harmony with the splendor and order of creation and with the glory of what is to come.

Presentation, in a sense, is being so thankful for the blessings God has bestowed on us that we cannot contain our joy. It is finding joy in the midst of any circumstance we are in, even when that circumstance is difficult.

Christians are not spared suffering, are not spared failures or defeats or illness or death, but we find joy in the faithfulness of God's promises. Proverbs 3:5-6 is an amazing promise that resonates so deeply in my soul that it should become my theme song. "Trust in the LORD with all your heart and lean not on your own understanding; in all your ways acknowledge Him, and he will make your paths straight." One translation puts it this way: "And He shall direct your paths."

I've talked about this invitation from as close as my living room and as far away as Budapest, I've counseled countless people with this fabulous message, and I've pulled myself from the brink of despair many times by praying those words of divine promise.

The good news of that promise is that true faith recognizes—and in all ways acknowledges—that the Lord's work is gloriously manifest in both good times and in storms. What distinguishes the Christian is the ability to accept the good and the bad with spiritual dependency and trust. "Trust in the LORD...lean not on your own understanding." There is a good deal of joy (and relief) in that.

Not feeling too joyful? Look to the sparrow or to the lilies of the field. Literally. Go outside and find joy in the expressions of God's revelation in His creation. (And while you are at it, take a gander at *His* presentation!)

> Can anyone think of believing in God without trusting Him? Is it possible to trust in God for the big things like forgiveness and eternal life, and then refuse to trust Him for the little things like clothing and food?
>
> —OSWALD C.J. HOFFMAN

Presenting "Presentation"

I have hosted meals for people who could buy our home with pocket change...and served them hot dogs and pork 'n beans. *That's* presentation.

I have taken a shawl from the closet and wrapped it round my shoulders and greeted guests with gusto. *That's* presentation.

I've made a $2 gift look like it came from Tiffany's, tied a red bandana around the Lab, put pretty stickers on note cards, filled my husband's lunch bucket with rose petals. *That's* presentation.

Presentation is a booster rocket for even the most positive attitude. It picks us up when we feel down. It soothes us, charges us, pleases us, and delights us. Let me make my case with some of Mom's wisdom.

One of the many lessons I've learned from my mother, a lesson that was jackhammered into my brain, was to always come home to a clean house. To this day, if I am leaving home for any appreciable time, a full sweep of the house leaves it ordered and clean. This is a valuable lesson! Nobody wants to come home to be greeted by drudgery. Everyone who wants to come home after an exhausting trip to find the beds made, the rooms neat, and the sink clean, raise your hand. A clean, ordered, and pretty house—*that* is presentation.

On dreary days I wander into our big, white kitchen and flip a switch that illuminates hundreds of tiny white lights. Some of the lights are tucked into long, green garlands on the tops of cupboards. Other lights are looped and wound on bundles of long sticks that run along the top of our tall kitchen windows as a valance. We buy these lights at Christmastime from the warehouse store (this is one item that sells fast, so waiting for after-Christmas sales doesn't work). The lights lift my spirits immeasurably. *That* is presentation.

We have a tall armoire in our dining room (from a used-furniture store). It's a big old thing with character galore. Four antique bean pots that were Joseph's mom's sit atop the cabinet, way up near the ceiling. At night the top of the cabinet looks dark, almost foreboding. Yet when we illuminate the small string of tiny amber lights we've strung among the pots, shazam! Little amenities, a whimsical touch, a dose of pizzazz.

Our homes are not only a remarkable expression of who we are—the condition and "presentation" of our homes also impact our own outlook. Consider the lights in our kitchen. For one lovely moment, when I walk into that room, my spirits are lifted no matter how dreary the day.

Many times, a simple transformation—as simple as shining some light on your life—can transform your entire outlook. The principle of presentation is enriching, especially in a fast-paced life that bogs down with stress and worry, because the first thing we jettison when we get serious is beauty. Without presentation, we get so immersed in the practical that we overlook the aesthetic.

Plain Jane or Plain Lazy?

Not everyone feels the way I do about presentation, and that is perfectly okay. "Presentation" will not cut the grocery bill, pay the kid's tuition, or put spare change in your pocket. But this principle can lift your spirits, make you smile, and occasionally make your dining room table rumba.

Some people have put their interest and energy into other issues: education, travel, caring for others, raising children. The same furniture in the same place, pictures in one spot on the wall for so long their imprints are permanently burned into the paint, curtains hanging since Moses was a baby. This is perfectly fine. Some people have other priorities.

Then there are those for whom patterned paper towels are about all the presentation they can stand. "Plain" is about as high on the style scale they care to go.

And then there are those who are intimidated by the notion of change or creativity. Many times people have come to me and said, "That's easy for you because you are creative!" My response? All you really have to do is open a drawer. If a shawl is in there, take it out. If a candle is in there, put it on the mantel and light it. If a pack of note cards is in there, use them (instead of scratch paper) to write a note of affection.

I sometimes wonder how much *I don't want to be bothered* is really behind *I don't think I can.*

So! For those of you who *do* want to bother, repeat after me: *Presentation is everything!*

Most of us like to put our best foot forward whether we are having someone over for dinner, hosting a book group or Bible study, or entertaining overnight guests. If we didn't, why do we go into a crazed cleaning mode just before company comes? I chuckle when I remember my childhood. We lived on a seldom-used street, and car lights in our driveway meant one thing—company. The minute lights would shine, Mom would marshal my sisters and me: *Company's coming!* We went into controlled frenzy. We shoved newspapers under couch cushions, flung clothes into closets, and summarily placed shoes back on our feet. Many a time someone was just using our driveway to turn around.

> *Smart Think:*
>
> Have you ever thought of hospitality as an expression of divine worship? That's what the Talmud says it is!

Because all of us can smile about our own frenzy when someone is coming, I will examine presentation mainly through the lens of hospitality.

Serving Others

Christians serve others as a demonstration of their devotion to Jesus. Hospitality toward others, as the Talmud says, can be an aspect of our worship. Jesus will someday say to the people on His right, "For I was hungry and you gave me something to eat, I was thirsty and you gave me something to drink, I was a stranger and you invited me in" (Matthew 25:35). One way our servanthood is manifested is in our graciousness to friends and strangers.

Imagine living life without the touch of a baby's hand, without a knowing glance across a room from the love of your life, without the hearty laugh of a grandfather, without the security that comes from the care and guidance of others. Imagine watching a sunset alone, eating at a favorite restaurant alone, receiving exciting news alone, receiving sorrowful news alone. Our life is enriched by those around us precisely because we know how vital a role other people play in our lives, either directly or indirectly. That awareness prompts us to recognize them, to thank them, and to love them. We celebrate the value of family and friends in our lives by honoring them—through hospitality.

It is especially important for us to tell those we love how much we value them. Every smile, touch, or hug is part of that expression and brings a message of tenderness and a feeling of well-being.

But as my mother would say, don't *tell* me, *show* me! Just how do you show honor to someone on that one limited income of yours?

The Adventures of Frugal Woman

I visited a woman whom I knew was down and out—*really* down and out. She offered me lunch. I panicked. I didn't want to take any of this woman's food, yet

I didn't want to embarrass her, so I graciously accepted. The woman had been to one of my talks just the weekend before. I watched from the corner of my eye as she prepared one-half of a tuna sandwich for me. She reached on her kitchen windowsill and grabbed a colorful wooden tulip. She wiped the flower with her dishtowel before she put it on the plate next to my meager sandwich, and brought it to me with a smile. *That* is presentation.

Breaking Bread

Having company for dinner? Make your table rumba! Dig through drawers and look on shelves. Present your food with flair. (I've heard that 80 percent of a dinner's success depends on presentation.) No more pork chop on a plate without pizzazz! Put it on a puddle of applesauce. Serve a super salad! Plop edible flowers on top. Be brave with biscuits! Bake them in a cast-iron skillet and serve them with chili con carne.

Another name for the Yates' dining room could be the "Shoestring Café," but to look at our table, you would think you were at the Ritz. Just the other day, Joseph and I hosted two recently married couples. We pulled all the stops to set a table that would dazzle the lovers and did what we could this side of heaven to present a "wedding feast." We served noodles. In full agreement with the 80-percent rule, much attention went to the table setting:

■ I arrayed clean (no stains) white tablecloth (a hand-me-down) with heavy, cut-glass candlesticks (from a warehouse store) on which white *dripless* candles (which I purchased on sale) flickered.

■ A glass vase with swirls of color (an heirloom) held fall flowers (from our garden).

- Fall leaves (from one of our bushes) rested near the base of the vase.

- Big, thick, white dishes served as chargers for the antipasto plates and later served as dinner plates. (They cost 50 cents each at an expensive store's closeout; these are our "everyday" dishes).

- Clear glass plates (from a dollar store) sat on each charger with a broadleaf fern (from a field) sandwiched in-between.

- We rolled crisp, white cloth napkins (purchased on sale) into silver napkin rings (that were a gift) and put them on each plate.

- Waterford crystal goblets ($7 each from a trip to Budapest) reflected the candlelight.

- Romantic music played softly in the background.

- Essential oil burned an hour before, putting a pleasant scent in the room.

- We dimmed the light over the table.

- Tea lights in an assortment of receptacles flickered throughout the dining room and living room.

- And then I served bread.

We set this table with a classy mix of expensive and down-right cheap accessories. Our theme was white with crystal, and just a touch of color. All we did was to start with the white tablecloth—our palette—and the rest fell into place merely by opening drawers.

The menu for this grand evening was simple and inexpensive: bread, antipasto, noodles with olive oil and garlic (maybe not the smartest thing to serve newlyweds), tea and cookies, and a stunning presentation using grapes and apples. The meal cost about $10. Here are some tips:

Bread

Bread is your number one ally when hosting any meal on a limited budget. In particular, the "breaking of bread" plays a vital role in getting people to relax and get to know one another. It is also filling. I have consistently found that if I load my company with a first course of bread and antipasto (or another appetizer of some sort), the main dish need not be extravagant, or even abundant. Frankly, guests *hope* the main meal isn't overboard because *they* have probably gone overboard with bread and butter. (We use nothing less than real butter, by the way.)

Making my own bread (with a fondness for the Italian foccacia) has become second nature. If I don't make my own, I purchase good, hearty breads from day-old racks and freeze them for future dinner parties. (Try not to use that weird, gooey stuff most markets pass off for Italian or French bread...what *is* that stuff, anyway? And what they call *garlic bread?* Ick!) In the oven toast thick slices of bread that have been lightly brushed with olive oil, and give each guest a peeled sliver of garlic to rub on their slice. Have fun, be different, and avoid chemicals from that weird stuff.

We often put olive oil and balsamic vinegar on the table and invite our guests to dip their bread in it in lieu of using butter. *For a variation,* serve mile-high baking powder biscuits with jam, cornbread with honey, tortillas rolled and steamed, or a heaping basket of hot pita.

Or instead of making breadsticks, make bread squiggles. Make or defrost bread dough. Roll the pieces into long, thin breadsticks. Turn the ends of the sticks into knots, squiggles, crooks—use your creative genius. Wash them with egg white and coat the ends with poppy, sesame, or caraway seeds. Bake them, but watch carefully so they don't burn. Serve these standing upright in a tall glass or flower vase.

Antipasto

This is so simple! Drain a can of garbanzo beans (you can buy them for 50 cents on sale) and mound a pile on a platter. Put something colorful next to the beans: thin-sliced red pepper (it's spendy out of season), cherry tomatoes cut in half, or dark olives. Let the items slop over into each other, and try to get something up in the air for dimension. We use what we have on hand for antipasto: sliced cucumber, radish, celery stuffed with cream cheese, mushrooms, asparagus, sliced apple, whatever cheese is in the fridge, and white beans (Don't use black beans! Oy, what a mess!). This first course of antipasto is intended to take a while. When we truly sit long and talk much, we begin to honor each other with good simple food and good will. We schedule dinners early so we have time to enjoy our company. A distinct benefit of antipasto is that it is prepared in advance and frees us to visit with friends. When assembling it, go for color, dimension, and the look of abundance. People eat with their eyes. I have learned that if a table looks full, guests will be full. To create a look of abundance, crowd food onto a plate or platter a tad too small. Another way to present antipasto is by piling lettuce leaves on a plate in a bit of a mound before scattering edibles all over.

Dessert

Go high, feast the eye. Try your level best to fill your table with selection (and stagger boxes if you must) to get serving plates at various heights on the table. Grapes are stars when it comes to presentation, especially when they cascade off the side of an elevated plate. Roll damp grapes in superfine sugar and freeze them. (Don't pay for superfine sugar. Run a bit of regular sugar in your blender or food processor.) Bold colors of tangerines, lemons and limes, apples, and bananas add a festive touch and fill space. Any candy or sliced cake on hand (freezer) adds more to the bounty. We buy gourmet cookies when we find them on sale and save them for the dessert table. We serve our "signature" candied nuts in champagne glasses (from the dollar store) and enjoy presenting our guests with a small cellophane bag of these nuts when they leave.

Incidentally, one time I almost bought cellophane bags through a popular TV show, the cellophane making such a smarter look than a sandwich baggie. Then I put the principle of creative genius to use: Onto the Internet I went, entering a search for "cellophane." I found the manufacturer, got their product catalogue, and bought cellophane bags of all sizes for next to nothing. I get a thrill when I enclose a basket of goodies in a big cellophane bag and tie it with raffia. Why, you'd think I stopped at an expensive store on my way home!

Aw, Nuts

2 cups walnuts

1 egg white

dash of water

1/4 cup sugar

1 teaspoon cinnamon

1/2 teaspoon nutmeg

Beat egg with water until frothy. Mix nuts with egg until fully coated, then drain nuts in colander for a couple of minutes. Mix sugar and spices in sturdy plastic baggie, add the nuts and thoroughly coat nuts by turning the closed baggie every which way. Put nuts on butter-greased tray and bake at 225 degrees for 2 hours. Every 20 minutes or so, stir nuts. When they are done...bet you can't eat just one!

Hey, Amigo!

Want to know how we got away with serving hot dogs and pork 'n beans to our company? Well, pull up a chair, pardner, and sit a spell...

Joe and I have been collecting blue-splatter enamelware for as long as we can remember. We have enough plates to host a mob, so we often do. These plates, bowls, cups, and spoons were found at thrift stores, and some were given as gifts by friends aware of our collection. Add to this collection my good fortune to stumble upon a going-out-of-business sale at a Mexican theme store. We now have huge, colorful serape tablecloths (80 percent off retail) and an assortment of terra cotta serving bowls. Olé! The perfect setting for hot dogs and pork 'n beans. Add cornbread in a cast-iron skillet or baking powder biscuits, piles of colorful citrus, a side order of kernel corn, and parfait glasses with mustard, ketchup, and chopped onion. Complete the look by winding a lariat around a *pink* cowboy boot candle (so help me, I found it at a dollar store) for a centerpiece, and you have a feast fit for any cowpoke or senorita to mosey your way.

Christmas Stroll

We live in a town famous for its Christmas grandeur. It's a small village that has a big heart during the holidays. Colorful lights hang on and off *everything* in our town. Using the principles of not wasting (the merriment of Main Street), and being creative (on an inexpensive night out), we sometimes invite friends from nearby towns to meet us *(dressed warmly)* at a park near the end of town. There we present our guests with hot cider we've brought in a thermos. Next we become Christmas elves and tour guides and lead them on a merry walk over the bedecked and bedazzled single-lane bridge and up the short hill into town. We do this on a weekend night when merchants fling open their doors and serve hot drinks and candy, when a horse-drawn sleigh jingles down the street, and when carolers belt some tunes. Afterwards we go home to hot chili and cornbread, and we belt some tunes of our own.

You'll Split Up over This

When is the last time you had a banana split? When is the last time you invited friends to your home for banana splits? We do this often, especially when winter begins to wear out its welcome and we are all starting to go a little stir-crazy.

We invested in a red-and-white-checked oilcloth (from the fabric store) to put on our table. Onto that we dump colorful sundae "sprinkles" (which we scoop up to save for the next split party) and set out parfait glasses filled with toppings, chopped nuts, and whipped cream. We scatter bananas on the table. We found banana split dishes at the dollar store. When everyone is at the table, we bring out the ice cream. Laughter and nostalgia immediately follow. Before long we are talking about our favorite "penny candy" and how we spent summers when we were kids.

The Adventures of Grim

If you read my first book, you know that I have an oddball friend called Grim. All my preaching about presentation must have really got to him because one day I received an emergency phone call. "I need *help!*"

I raced to his home and found an unusual scene: Grim was dressed in an old frilly apron and *cooking;* his kitchen looked like a tornado had just passed through.

"Grim," I said, "what is wrong?" He needed help decorating his table, he said. "For *what?*" I asked. Grim grinned. He had set out two plastic plates, two Styrofoam cups, two sets of plastic utensils, and two Dairy Queen paper napkins.

"Grim," I teased, "are you expecting company?" He looked at his feet and turned red…Grim had a girlfriend! And he was preparing Valentine's dinner for her—tuna casserole, but it was a start.

I rolled up my sleeves and ran to the bathroom. I searched his trash for two cardboard rollers from toilet paper, raced to the kitchen and ripped off two pieces of aluminum foil. I ran out to my car (where the groceries for *my* Valentine's dinner were) and grabbed a sack of chocolate kisses. I loaded each toilet paper roll with kisses and rolled them in foil so the ends could be crimped and tied with red curly ribbon. Then I stuck a Valentine sticker on each roll.

"What's her name, Grim?" I asked, as I reached for his red Magic Marker. He swooned. "Grace." (I could only think she would need a *lot* of grace to date this strange ranger...) I printed her name and his above the stickers and used them for place settings. With the red pen I drew hearts all over the cups, and then I turned the napkins inside out and rolled them, tying them with more of the curly ribbon. I found a lemon in his fridge, cut it in half, hollowed it out, and put votive candles in each half. I stuck heart stickers all over his folded white sheet tablecloth and scattered even more of the kisses on the table.

"So, Grim," I said, "tell me about this woman." He showed me to the door.

～ ～ ～

Hospitality Tips

■ When guests arrive after a long trip, have homemade soup waiting for them. A grand, big dinner is a waste of time and money on your exhausted visitors. A salad, a hot, nourishing soup, and a chunk of bread fits the bill nicely and prepares them for a comfortable night's rest. Tuck them into bed with chamomile tea.

■ Bake and decorate cookies and invite friends or family to celebrate Tuesday, or the seventeenth, or the color green. Invent a celebration.

▣ Want a no-cost idea to use as a pick-me-up for a friend down in the dumps? Drive over to the person's home, rummage around in the fridge, and *you* make dinner. Call it the Blue Plate Special. Make it on toast if you have to! Wash the dishes and play cards afterwards.

▣ Want to make your children think they are the most special kids in the universe? Put ice cream in a wide-mouth thermos and freeze it the night before you put it in their lunch box. Be sure to include a spoon.

▣ Use those hand towels taking up room in your linen closet. Tie a few together with a pretty ribbon and place them on the bed or in the bath of your guest visitor.

▣ An inexpensive floral arrangement for your guest's room could be a huge bouquet of florist greens with baby's breath interspersed. It is long lasting, too. Just be sure to remove the leaves from the part of the stem that is immersed in water. Crisscross Scotch tape on the mouth of a vase and insert long-stemmed flowers in the holes to keep your arrangement from leaning against the sides.

Table Tips

▣ Twinkle lights aren't just for cupboard tops and windows. String them on the table. Tape the electric cord to the floor, tie it to the table leg (careful not to mar the furniture finish), and light up the night. I've done this for an autumn birthday party. I strung red lights among tiny gourds and pumpkins scattered on the table. Wow.

▣ Use a quilt as a tablecloth. Be sure to think twice about this—use this route when you are serving "safe" food and drink.

Jazz Up Your Front Door

Want to put pizzazz in your palace and make your home inviting? Jazz up the front door! Keep two thoughts in mind: 1) Presentation is everything, and 2) first impressions go a long way. What can you do?

- Polish or replace all the hardware or the doorknob.

- Paint the door. I don't know about you, but my eye wanders to any home that has a different (and agreeable) color to the front door. It's practically *begging* me to stop and visit a while.

- Add a door knocker.

- Add painted wood or brass house numbers. By the way, having a well-marked house with easy-to-read numbers makes a lot of sense in case of emergency when firefighters, police officers, or paramedics are trying to find you.

- Add a doormat. Careful, though! Some mats simply trap moisture underneath and rot wooden decks. In our case, where our outside entrance is not protected from the weather, we went with a heavy-duty rubber mat that has cutouts throughout, giving it a lacy look. It adds elegance, does its thing, and doesn't rot the porch boards.

- Hang a wreath. Put seasonal wreaths on your door! (Maybe make one with twinkle lights...outdoor-approved lights, by the way.) Is anything more inviting?

Presentation in the Garden

So how *does* your garden grow? I once was asked to speak to a garden club and came up with these ten suggestions for presentation. What is gardening, anyway, but presentation?

1. Mounds in the garden look better than completely level ground. Just as you try to stagger heights in your antipasto or in your dessert presentation, try to get a few different heights in your garden.

2. Use rock instead of timbers. This is especially wise in veggie gardens, where you would not want "treated" timber anywhere near your food. If you are lucky to live in a rocky terrain, you have unlimited free material.

3. Make paths of flat stone. Please don't make your path straight! We are to *walk* a straight path, and the Lord will *make* our path straight, but when you design a path through your garden or to your door, make it a bit winding. It will look more natural. If you doubt me, follow the paths of wild animals. They meander.

4. Hollow out a stump and plant Virginia creeper. Buy the creeper in the fall when perennials go on sale.

5. Buy plants that can become houseplants in the winter. Or learn how to care for them outside so they survive inclement weather.

6. Don't be afraid of open space. It is the look of nature.

7. Don't plant everything in a straight line. Group things in threes for a more natural look.

8. Use just about anything as a container. I once planted a rooted clipping of ivy in a teacup on a saucer. It was a lovely gift for a friend who missed the prolific ivy of her childhood home.

9. "Paint" with flowers. One expert discourages putting several plants of different hues in one container. She feels one color per container presents a more stunning look.

10. Pluck off anything dead. Just make certain it is dead before you pluck! A friend tells the story how she conversed once with her neighbor, all the while busying herself "plucking" dead petunias off her neighbor's floral display. Imagine her chagrin when she learned she was plucking budding new flowers before her neighbor's eyes!

> For God giveth to a man that is good in his sight wisdom, and knowledge, and joy.
> —ECCLESIASTES 2:26

CHAPTER 11

To God Be the Glory

O LORD, thou art my God; I will exalt thee, I will praise thy name; for thou hast done wonderful things; thy counsels of old are faithfulness and truth.

—ISAIAH 25:1

Soli Deo Gloria

*A*nd so we come to a close. My fervent hope is that the end of this book signals a beginning for you, a beginning filled with confidence and the conviction that regardless of your income, you have power to triumph over your circumstance, if only with a "new and improved" outlook.

Armed with new skills, a half-full attitude, and some old-fashioned grit, you are now better prepared for challenges that come your way. These skills may not represent a "magic wand" solution to your situation, but they will work together toward making your circumstance more tolerable.

Throughout these pages I've talked about how attitude can propel you toward either success or failure when you are troubled by your limited income.

I've challenged you to try to live within established budgetary guidelines.

I've demonstrated the value of sound organization of possessions and time.

I've implored you to become a savvy consumer and to learn prices.

I've prodded you to roll up your sleeves and to save money by doing things yourself.

I've appealed to you to practice the critical principle of using what you have.

I've begged you not to waste.

I've shown you how to find and use your creativity when looking for the path of least expenditure.

And I hope I've inspired you to repeat after me: Presentation is everything.

All of these principles act together in syncretism, yet none is possible without the grace and mercy of our holy God. With that in mind, I now give you the overriding principle, the super precept, the last and greatest rule that spreads over all the rest: To God be the honor and glory!

The Love of Money

Money is neither good nor bad. It happens to be the currency we use for trade. The purpose of this book has been to empower you to approach money management with an enthusiastic and responsible attitude.

As Christians, our primary stewardship responsibility is to reach others with the Good News and to live for the glory of God. As I mentioned before, that responsibility includes the wise use of the gifts God has given us. Other folks should benefit from our wise use of those gifts. Stewardship responsibility also includes our attitude and Christian witness as we manage financial affairs.

Have you ever considered that you bring God glory when you pay your bills on time, spend wisely, prepare for the unexpected, plan for your future, tithe, and help others?

In their book *Smart Money,* Jerry and Ramona Tuma and Tim LaHaye ask: How can we effectively witness to non-Christians if they see no difference between our lives and theirs? If others don't see peace, freedom, love, and joy in our lives, what will draw them to Jesus?

He Is the Potter, After All

We are the clay, right? Made and molded in His image. Blessed. Loved.

What do we really know about God's love? We know it must be a very big love, indeed. We also know that God's love is always seeking that which is best for us, even when His love seems unjustified. We know that *love itself* is the very essence of God, and when we love as He loves, He fills the space in our hearts with light and grace. This is "attitude supreme." Combine this attitude with diligence to follow the counsel of Scripture and we will triumph.

Smart Think:

Does the way I live speak louder than words?

We will triumph. *We,* whose dreams may have gone sour, yet are told to give thanks. *We,* whose very households mirror His created order, and are told to depend. *We,* whose fears and uncertainties threaten to snuff out our very breath, but are told to trust.

Financial security must never ever become the overriding goal of our trust. All the money in the world will not replace the certainty and security that is found in God alone. We trust Him to guide our path, we trust Him to provide for our needs just as He provides for lilies and sparrows, and we trust Him to know what is best for us. Even (or especially) with regard to money.

When we remind ourselves that God owns everything, the matter of caring for His possessions—our stewardship—takes on new meaning. But God isn't a grumpy old tightwad! His Word provides us with guidance for successful living. The Bible is filled with the story of redemption, for sure, but it is also filled with admonition and instruction. If we are faithful to Scripture, God will be faithful and true and will help us as we muddle through our daily affairs. When we take the Bible's counsel, we are in right relationship with the owner of all things. Caring for His possessions is a joy. If we understand from the start that we are administrators of God's provision, we are more responsible and accountable for what He has entrusted to us.

God expects increase of whatever He has invested in us. Our gifts, our possessions, and our relationships are ours to use only for a time. A day for settling accounts is coming. Why, *we* are not even our own! We were bought with a price. Many times things go wrong in life when we lose sight of this truth.

> ## Smart Think:
>
> No matter what He has given me, I am like a tenant. The true owner of all things is my Creator God. He has loaned me my life, my family, my skills, and all of my resources. He calls me to manage those things in a way that honors Him.

Honor Him

Honor. Curious, isn't it? The commandment given to us about parents is to *honor* our mother and our father. This commandment from a parent who never sleeps, who never takes His eyes off our affairs, who never ceases to love.

The Adventures of Frugal Woman

Many years ago I encountered a bitter man. During a counseling session he vented decades of pain and anger in my direction. Much of the man's hurt seemed justified—his parents abused and abandoned him when he was young. A new Christian, the man railed against the fourth commandment. How could a loving God expect us to overcome our personal history all at once and skip down the street singing accolades to Mommy and Daddy? It was too much for him, and he was deeply troubled because of it.

"You know," I replied, "God knows your heart. And though He surely wants your pain and anger—and unforgiveness—to be replaced by His mercy, grace, and forgiveness, He asks now that you honor your parents. You can do that by living as godly a life as you can. If you can muster that, the Holy Spirit will have His way with you, and love and forgiveness may come after all."

~ ~ ~

How can you honor God by living wisely—and well—on one income?

You honor Him by having an attitude of thankfulness for His blessings and an attitude of earnest obedience as you strive to be more like Him.

You honor Him when you show self-control and live responsibly and satisfied within the circumstance you are in.

You honor Him when you maintain order and harmony in your surroundings and recognize that He who is timeless has created time for you to use wisely.

You honor Him when you consider prices and purchase skillfully (Proverbs 31).

You honor Him when you consider the ant and take control of unnecessary expenses by doing things yourself.

You honor Him when you recognize the bounty of your life and live content within that bounty. Or when you dig up your buried talent and use it to His glory.

You honor Him especially when you are not greedy, gluttonous, or wasteful of His providence, and you recognize the needs of others.

You honor Him when you turn to Him for help when trying to find the path of least expenditures.

You honor Him when you remember that He who created the world and all that is in it also created (and mandated!) festivals for celebrating and feasting on His faithfulness.

I can be calm and free from care on any shore, since God is there.

—MADAME JEANNE GUYON

Go Godward; Thou Wilt Find a Path

Isn't that a lovely Russian proverb? It is a wonderful sentiment that I would like to leave you with.

I've tried my best to "show *and* tell," so to speak. I've unabashedly shared my successes and blunders. I've endeavored to help you turn your hardships into dancing.

Within this book I've written about how some of our financial problems seem like the on-ramp of the Indy 500; I've written about the path of least expenditure, and about the Lord leading your path. My prayer is that as you turn Godward your path will rise up to meet you, that it is a little less bumpy, and that you will never skin your knee again.

Smart Think:

Life is change; growth is optional.

He has showed you, O man, what is good. And what does the LORD require of you? To act justly and to love mercy and to walk humbly with your God.

—MICAH 6:8

Soli Deo Gloria

Budget in a Nutshell

1. A budget is a state of mind. It is a determination to not be controlled by every whim and fancy that comes our way. Fifty percent of what we spend we spend impulsively, and 25 percent of what we spend is on things *we do not need*. Be honest. Track your money. For the most part, people spend unnecessarily. Decide you are going to cut impulse in half, and you are ahead of the pack already.

2. Don't think that because you are paying your bills that you are in good shape financially. Are you tithing? Are you contributing to others in some way? Do you have at least three months' salary squirreled away for emergencies, not to mention the savings plan for college, marriage, and retirement?

3. Talk with others in your family and make this a joint effort. Bring all the bills (and income statements) to the table. Do not bring hammers, fly swatters, bats, or boxing gloves. Talk about your financial income and outgo. Use coins to demonstrate to the younger children without scaring them. If you include your children in this discussion, be sure to assure them that you will take care of them, regardless of the circumstances.

4. You've heard it over and over and over again: Get rid of as many credit cards as you can. Remember that credit-card debts are easier made than paid.

5. Invest in a budget workbook and challenge yourself to stick to it two weeks at a time. If there is another adult in the house, become mutually accountable.

6. Don't cut your throat. Ease into changes. Practice the tips in this book. Turn your determination to save into an adventure, not a tight-fisted plunge into personal depravity. Do little things such as skipping a week at the grocery market, buying your espresso every *other* day, and going to the park instead of the mall for recreation.

7. If you are in over your head, pray. And then take action. Every single *second* you avoid your problem, you are getting in deeper. A sure sign that you are in trouble is your reluctance to open the mail.

Savvy Strategies and Tips When Purchasing Food

Super Gimmicks of Super Markets

▪ Highest-priced items will always be at eye level (pay close attention to where the gaily colored cereal boxes are located—right at kid level, aren't they?)

▪ End-of-aisle displays are *not* always the best buy. Often you can beat the price if you go down that aisle. Also, this is a place where grocers might put soon-to-expire items.

▪ Grouping is a major gimmick. What does that mean? Putting displays together that include several different items: chips with pop, salad dressings with produce, toppings with ice cream.

▪ "Grab me" displays of precut fruits and veggies...tsk tsk tsk—not very frugal to let someone else cut your cantaloupe!

▪ This one will fool you every time—a special display of gourmet cheeses. You can probably buy the same or similar cheeses in the dairy case for much less. You aren't still buying preshredded or precut cheese, are you? C'mon, now!

- This is the all-time, oldest gimmick in the book— putting milk way in the back of the store so you have to trudge past everything else to get to it.

Fight Those Grocery Bill Blues

- A little known secret: Most stores will break up bunches of produce to sell you a smaller amount. If you need a little bit of something, such as celery or cabbage, just ask.

- Try less-expensive "house" brands. You may be in for a nice surprise.

- Stay clear of the gourmet section.

- Stay clear of processed foods: preseasoned chicken, stuffed pork chops, coleslaw mix.

- Factor in the weight of bones when buying meat.

- Never ever buy a dairy product without checking expiration date.

- Stock up on genuine bargains—*if you will use what you buy*.

- Ignore the new and improved stuff. These ads always slay me. Like, the merchandisers are admitting that their products were inferior before?

- Stay clear of convenience foods (like sliced cheese).

- Buy in season.

- Back off on the meat.

- Back off on the stuff that isn't good for you in the first place. Try to drink water instead of pop half the time and you will save money, calories, and health. Especially bone health.

- Read labels. Ingredients are listed by weight.

- Buy only what you eat and eat what you buy.

- Shop with a list and stick to it. Leave a couple of spaces blank for planned impulse.

- Shop alone. Try not to take the kids with you.

- Rumor has it that the cereal aisle is the most expensive aisle in the grocery store.

- Here is a super tip! Weigh the prepackaged meats and fruits and veggies. You may be surprised to find a five pound sack of spuds weighing in at almost six pounds.

- Things in bags usually cost less than things in boxes.

Conservation Tips

Energy Consumption

When Cooking Indoors:

- Don't preheat your oven unless a recipe calls for it.

- Turn off the oven just before the food is completely cooked.

- Use pots that fit the size of the heating element.

- Keep lids on pots at all times.

- If you have reflector pans, be sure they are clean.

- Try to bake more than one thing if the oven will be on.

Around the House:

- Keep your water thermostat at 120 degrees.

- Use shades and blinds that filter out high levels of sunlight. Keep them closed on the sunny sides of your home in summer, open in winter.

- Keep your heat pump thermostat set on 78 degrees or higher. Each degree you set it lower costs about 3 percent more in energy costs.

■ Keep conditioned air in the house by using exhaust fans in baths and kitchens only when absolutely necessary.

■ For maximum comfort, use ceiling fans to keep cooled air circulating throughout your home.

■ Keep out extra heat by turning off unneeded lights around the house, by cooking meals outdoors on the grill, or by using your microwave.

■ Take short warm showers instead of long hot baths.

■ If you have a dishwasher, use the energy-saver features and let the dishes air dry. This saves time and money and keeps unnecessary heat out of the kitchen.

■ If you depend on a window air conditioning unit to keep cool, install one on the north or shaded side of the house to keep it from fighting the sun's heat. Also, close off rooms that are not in use.

■ Check the filter on your heat pump or central air conditioning system. Cleaning or replacing filters monthly is one of the best ways to keep your unit operating efficiently.

Precycling Tips

Precycle newspapers. Do you receive more than one paper? Why? Can you read your paper during a break at work or at a nearby library? Can you share a paper with a neighbor? Can you satisfy your need to know by watching the evening news or by listening to the radio?

Precycle pop and juice containers. Drink water.

Precycle anything made microwave-ready. Do not buy it.

Precycle much in your grocery cart. Buy bulk. Bring your own containers if possible. If not, use paper bags and reuse them for lunch containers. Save money by buying smart, and reduce waste as a bonus. Write this on an index card: Shopping cart = garbage pail. Tape that to the handle of your cart next time you shop.

Precycle food leftovers. Make a compost pile.

Water Conservation

▓ Repair leaky faucets.

▓ Keep a bottle of water in the fridge to avoid running the tap too long.

▓ Cover your swimming pool when you're not using it to prevent evaporation. Do not fill it too high so the water doesn't splash out.

▓ Plant native outdoor plants that need less water.

▓ Do not cut your lawn short in hot weather.

▓ Use drip irrigation and a water timer. Water your yard at night.

▓ Consider low-consumption faucets.

▓ Use a vegetable brush and short bursts of water rather than letting your tap run.

▓ Use an electric razor for shaving.

▓ Install a low-flow showerhead. You will save 20 gallons every five minutes. Faucet aerators and efficient showerheads mean big savings. Some power and water companies supply showerheads free.

▓ Use the sink stopper. Do not let hot water run down the drain while shaving or washing dishes.

▓ Always use cold water in the garbage disposal.

▓ Use cold water for washing clothes whenever possible.

■ Reduce the amount of flush water by filling and sealing two plastic, one-quart bottles with sand or rocks and placing them in the tank, *away from the flushing mechanism*. Do not use bricks (they damage your mechanism).

■ If your home is unoccupied for more than three days and your water heater is protected from freezing, turn it off.

■ Clean sediment buildup in your water heater to increase its efficiency.

■ Wash your car with short bursts from the hose.

Cynthia Yates

Cynthia's talks, seminars, and retreats have entertained and inspired audiences for nearly two decades. Her topics range from money management to marriage enrichment, from trusting God to walking as children of light.

Her radio show, *Spirit of the Age,* covered cultural and spiritual issues from a Christian perspective and aired for eight years.

She has been a popular speaker with youth groups and has a particular heart for the young.

Contact Cynthia at
www.cynthiayates.com

Books You Can Believe In™
from Harvest House Publishers

Money Management for Those Who Don't Have Any
James L. Paris

If your financial problems need solutions fast, this guide will provide it. Discover over 200 strategies for budgeting, reducing expenses, borrowing wisely, lowering insurance fees and taxes, and even having fun without "fun" money.

Life Management for Busy Women
Elizabeth George

Elizabeth George—speaker, teacher, and bestselling author of *A Woman After God's Own Heart*®—admits to being a disorganized, goalless woman when she was in her 20s. Over the decades, God has taught her how to...

- live each day God's way
- take charge of busyness and find a balanced life
- be a better steward of resources

This unique sourcebook will strike a chord with women hungering to live orderly lives that are a testimony to their faith.

Keep It Simple for Busy Women
Emilie Barnes

Elegant and joyous, this book is an oasis of serenity in a woman's stress-filled life. Devotions for every weekday, arranged by month, offer inspirational thoughts, short prayers, and simple pleasures.

More Hours in My Day
Emilie Barnes

This bestseller speaks to people who long for a few extra minutes to take a breath, get focused, and get organized. Emilie helps bring order to everything from paperwork to prayer lives.